Dedicated to my family and friends for their
constant support and encouragement
to stay the course.

To my brothers and sisters, my lifelong
teachers.

Dad. I did it!

To my Ali. There are no words anymore,
only love.

WHO ARE YOU:
Become
THE VERY BEST
U THAT U CAN BE

KEVIN L. MCCRUDDEN

Published by AudioInk
P.O. Box 1775
Issaquah, WA 98027
www. AudioInk.com

Distributed by AudioInk

For ordering information, please contact AudioInk +14255266480

Cover Design by AudioInk
Interior Design by AudioInk
Interior Artwork created by Ron Weickart, www.network-graphics.com, 1+6312656086

Publisher's Cataloguing-in-Publication

    McCrudden, Kevin L.
        Who Are U? Become the Very Best U That U Can Be
        p. cm.
        PCN/LCCN 2012937638
        ISBN: 978-1-61339-257-7

        1. SELF-HELP / General 2. SELF-HELP / Motivational & Inspirational 3. SELF-HELP / Personal Growth / General

Printed in the United States of America

For further information contact AudioInk +14255266480 or email support@AudioInk.com

"Kevin McCrudden's new book revises and revitalizes Abraham Maslow's hierarchy of needs to apply directly to our current culture. His book is insightful, innovative and in tune with the rapid changes in our society. His emphasis on acceptance of difference and gratitude for the kindnesses in life is most needed in our complicated, fast paced world. I think Dr. Maslow would welcome Kevin's creative manuscript and approve the need for a new, creative view of human nature".

- Dr. Arthur Ciaramaccoli

Clinical Psychologist / Instructor Harvard Medical School

Author: *"TheCurseoftheCapable"*

www.thecurseofthecapable.com

"Kevin continues to motivate, inspire and educate. This new book and the creation of "The 21st Century Multidimensional Hierarchy of Needs" is an extension of his unique view of the world and an appropriate follow up to "National Motivation & Inspiration Day." I applaud Kevin's ongoing commitment to motivating and inspiring America and America's youth."

- Warren Struhl

Chief Inspiration Officer @ Successories.com

Author of *"StartingThemUp"*

www.Successories.com

"If America is looking for change, they need look no further than Mr. Motivation, Kevin McCrudden. He has proven once again to be a leader in the motivation and personal development industry. From his leadership role in the media industry to his creation of National Motivation & Inspiration Day; and The American Motivation Awards to his New 21st Century Multidimensional Hierarchy of Needs. Kevin's unique vision continues to produce results that nobody else has created before him."

-Steve Maraboli

President - A Better Today

Internet Talk Radio Host ~ Empowered Living with Steve Maraboli

www.SteveMaraboli.com

Table of Contents

INTRODUCTION

If you review the history of mankind there have been some amazingly inspired thinkers: Aristotle. Archimedes. DaVinci. Einstein. Freud. Newton. Nostradamus. Shakespeare. Plato and so many more.

And of course there were some that were very motivated to be successful, such as: Copernicus. Galileo. Marco Polo and Christopher Columbus, men that were driven, *motivated* to find what they were seeking.

And finally were those that had both, the "magic" or imagination to dream or think of great ideas and then the motivation and determination to see it through…to successfully achieve their dreams that changed mankind forever. Michelangelo. Benjamin Franklin. Thomas Edison. Henry Ford. The Wright Brothers and many more.

> "Whatever the mind of man can perceive and believe,
> it can achieve."
> *~Napoleon Hill~*

These men were inspired to find new lands, invent new ideas, create amazing images and are responsible for the advancement of our society in many ways.

> "If you think you can or you think you can't, you're
> probably right."
> *~ Henry Ford ~*

My question is, though; how can we advance so far as a society and yet we are not advancing the development of our minds and its utilization on a grand scale nor are we developing them at an earlier age or *evolving* more quickly. For example, the emotional and hormonal challenges associated with teens are the same challenges faced centuries ago.

> "The challenges of today cannot be solved with the same thinking that created them."
>
> ~ *Einstein* ~

As the youngest male in an Irish immigrant family of eight, I suppose I may have a different definition of "motivation" than most. However, I believe like many that true motivation comes from within. That internal voice or energy source that pushes you to want more, be more and accomplish more, but is that genetic or learned?

Young adults typically study the "Nature vs. Nurture" argument in Freshman Biology…do we know which wins in the end? What abilities, skills and talents do we have genetically from our parents and what is enhanced, developed or destroyed from how and where we are raised?

These are questions that have been debated for years, however, there is one constant. In all of time there is one consistent truth about change and development. Change is constant and "development" occurs all around us, however, there is one place that "change" is controlled and that is with each human being.

Each and every human being has a choice to change or not change; accept the "status quo" or do something different, accept their own human failings or work diligently to create a different reality. Every single human being has that ability and power to choose.

So, this book is dedicated to U. Do U know the steps to create a new reality? Do U know who U are? What U are made of? What is "nature / genetic" and what is "nurture / developed?"

If U choose to, by the time U are done with this book, U will find a new reality and a new U!

U ! What makes You …U? "To thyne own self be true!"

The study of psychology and behavior is as old as man itself. The curiosity of Eve. The judgment of Adam. Even if you look at Evolutionary Theory you can see how animals watch with curiosity and measure and judge each other's behaviors and movements. There are signals for fight or flight or mating calls, amongst a million other messages and signals.

So, our nature as human beings, as Homo sapiens, is developed by what things?

The most fundamental is genetics. You are the offspring of two other human beings, Homosapiens…what did they pass on to you?

Are you tall, short, fat, skinny, slow, fast, intelligent, dumb, athletic, spastic, clever, witty, driven, lazy, stable, unstable, healthy, unhealthy are you psychologically sound or is there something "wrong" with how you process information before there is one particle of information given to you at birth.

There has been much study of the human genome and I will not venture to discuss this, but suffice to say that much of who you are is given to you genetically.

Keep in mind, with this very statement, probably half the people that will read this book will disagree. They will insist that the biggest influence in your life is not your genetics, but what you do with it. Hence the ongoing debate, which prevents forward movement in any one direction.

> "I am convinced that life is 10% of what happens to me and 90% of what I do with it." *C. Swindoll*

So now what?

There are incredible athletes that "have it all" that get injured or retire and become "losers" or lose their way in life.

There are some of the most beautiful women in the world who succumb to drugs and promiscuity and prostitution.

There are people born into wealth, a literal *silver spoon* in their mouth that become failures and commit suicide.

And there are people that come from absolute poverty and have literally nothing that become leaders!

Do you ever ask yourself, how? Why? Why do these people make the decisions they make and how do they become who they become? Well, stop right there!

> "When you point your finger at someone...there
> are three fingers pointing back at you."

When you ask those questions of others, it is the very question you should be asking yourself. What decision did I make to get here? How have I gotten to where I am and how can I get to where I want to go? Rather than "judging" OJ Simpson, Britney Spears, Bernie Madoff or Lindsay Lohan, what "mistakes" are you making that are preventing you from getting where you want to go and what "positive" things are you doing to be "successful" in getting where you want to go?

"If you have no destination any road will get you where you are going!" With this said, we should have a "higher expectation" for ourselves and for others. When we "judge" others, we are simply stating that their "belief system" or "morals" or "mores" are not in line or in tune with our belief system and therefore we "judge." Just like other animal species, we do watch and judge to determine if something is a danger to our own self-preservation or to the things, property or people that are important to us. If they are considered a danger, then there is a potential conflict or "attack."

Either on them personally or symbolically or verbally, which indicates disproval and rejection of them and their behavior.

So then. Back to the question at hand, "what makes you…U?"

We understand the power of genetics, however, you can take the strongest physical specimen ever born and not feed it or take care of it when it's born and it will die. Regardless of how strong the genetic code of an infant, if it is not taken care of properly, it will perish.

Therefore, the difficult argument begins. Once a child is born, how much of its environment is enhancing and strengthening its "genetic strengths" and what is being done in its environment to detract or take away from its genetic strengths, which may take away from the overall potential of the child or will it feed the fire it needs to be "successful?" It is impossible to think of raising a child in a "perfect" environment and never making a mistake, because the challenges and issues faced by some of the most successful people in the world is exactly what have caused them to succeed at a higher level. If they had not had challenges or issues at an earlier age, they may not have evolved or become who they did otherwise.

As you can see, these are very difficult questions and vary by as many people as there are in the world, because every human experience is our own. Children that come from the very same homes with the very same upbringing can have very different feelings and results from their upbringing.

Once again, coming from a family of eight children with alcoholic parents, I can attest that the events of our home had different effects on different personalities within the family; however, there are some themes and similarities. There is also a growing study of "Birth Order" and where you were born within your family. Everyone knows the old generalization about being "the middle child." Well? How much of that is actually true and how much of those generalizations apply for *middle children* and what assumptions are largely incorrect.

As you can see, it is very difficult to determine which argument is correct, "Nature vs. Nurture," and hopefully I have painted an accurately twisted and distorted picture of how hard it is to determine what has the bigger influence on the development of a person.

So. We come back to U again.

Only you know what you think or feel about the development of your past and how you see the results of how you were brought up. You can clearly see what some of your "genetics" are and what you get from which parent, but that's still not the end, because, as you know, there are millions of people in therapy to determine why they are "not healthy" or to "work out their issues." And if you do not know the genetic makeup of your parents or have spent time watching them and get to see those characteristics come out of you at some point in your adult life, don't worry, that's not the end of the world either.

Counseling and therapy are critically important and I would never make light of their importance. Finding the right therapist can be like finding a flashlight in the dark. Someone that can shine the light on your darkest fears and insecurities to help you overcome and increase your personal success.

In many circumstances, the right counselor will help you find the answers you have right inside. A place that I hope to help you find. A deeper sense of self understanding and self belief…a place where you know that goodness and ability lay, but you have just been too afraid or insecure to find it.

My dream for U, is that once you have read this book, maybe once, maybe ten times, that you find parts of you that you have lost or maybe never knew existed and thereby find peace, happiness, security, joy and serenity in your life.

Serenity Prayer

*"God, grant me the serenity to accept the things that
I cannot change; Courage to change the things I can;
and the wisdom to know the difference."*

One of the greatest and simplest prayers that I know and have ever heard. It breaks down the complexity of life into three simple concepts.

Grant me **"serenity."** What a beautiful word. Can you imagine finding "serenity?" Having "serenity" in your daily life…a way of living?

"…to **ACCEPT** the things **I CANNOT CHANGE**" and "**COURAGE** to change the things I can."

Acceptance. How often do we find acceptance of things in our heart? How often do you find "serenity" through "acceptance" that you "cannot change something?" I will admit that this is hard, because for many that strive for achievement, the overachievers or "A personalities" as they are described, it is very difficult to accept something that you cannot change or have control over.

"Courage" is such a great word and one that is misused so frequently. As individuals we must define what "courage" is to us. Is it the courage of a soldier or a fire fighter going into the flames to save someone's life? Is that "courage?" Is it a politician having the "courage" to make a certain vote? What exactly is courage to you? Does it take "courage" to stop smoking, over eating, drinking, cheating, lying, stealing or abusing? One of the greatest challenges anyone ever faces is to "change themselves" and it takes tremendous personal courage to say that you have "failed." Whether it's failing yourself or others. It does, in fact, take a great deal of courage to take an introspective look at yourself to determine a long term behavior that needs to change and you must find the "courage" to acknowledge it and then the fortitude to change it. Politicians that use the word "courage" to describe anything they do is an insult to those that actually do have courage.

…"and the **WISDOM** to know the difference."

Finally, "wisdom." **"Wisdom"** comes in many forms. I love sitting and speaking to older people because they have perspective and "wisdom." Experience can bring with it amazing forethought and wisdom, however, how many times have you heard some of the most profound, simple and wise comments come from a child?

"…from the mouth of babes…"

The power and simplicity of the Serenity Prayer are words to live by. If each individual literally and actually listened to and performed based on this concept, the world would be a much better place.

One of the beauties of the Serenity Prayer is not only its simplicity, but also its personal accountability. When taken literally, it states specifically for each individual to establish a set of goals and parameters to find "serenity." Now, that might not be everyone's goal, but to find a personal sense of peace and serenity about one's self and your life. That seems like a pretty reasonable goal in life.

Spiritual "serenity" may not be your goal. Do you have one? What is your goal in life? "What do you want to be when you grow up?" Many will say they want to be "rich." Well, how do you define, "rich." Some will say that, literally, it means "a lot of money." Well, that's great and you can debate how much is a lot of money, based on where and when you live, but the next question may be the most important. How do you get there? How are you going to "earn" your millions or billions? This is incredibly important, because most people, children and adults refer to it as "making money," when in fact it is how you "earn money." Unless you work at the US Treasury and actually "print" / "make" the money, we all have to take some action and work in some way to "earn" money.

This is why I say to young adults and young professionals just in the work world, "find what you love to do and the money will follow."

"Do what you love and the money will follow."

That's right. It can be that simple. I suggest to young adults and young professionals that if they do what they love, they have a competitive edge. If you love what you do, it makes it easier to get up early and stay up late and to work hard and long hours. Someone that hates what they are doing will be miserable getting up early and staying up late to do the same work and at some point in time will quit or not be able to give the same kind of effort you do, because you have a passion and they do not.

So, who are U…and who do U want to become? What is your "destiny" here on earth?

In August of 2001 my good friend David and I were having lunch at the Brickhouse Brewery in Patchogue, Long Island. David was one of my most trusted advisors when I ran for office several years earlier and continues to be a good friend and treasured advisor.

I was sharing with him an idea I had for a day dedicated to "motivation and inspiration." My concern was that it seemed more people were living lives without direction. I was hearing far too many people use the phrase, "same shit, different day." I used to think, "Wow, how pathetic." And some of the young people I knew and saw seemed to lack direction and passion.

In the very same room there happened to be representatives from our local Congressman's office, who, at the time, was

Congressman Felix Grucci from the world renowned fireworks family.

Little did I know the timing of my thoughts and actions would lead me to become the only motivational and leadership speaker in America to have a day of recognition passed by The United States Congress. Nor could I anticipate the impact of September 11, 2001.

Prior to 9/11, the concept of a day dedicated to "motivation and inspiration" might not have seemed important or worthwhile enough to bring for a Congressional vote. Fortunately and unfortunately, it came to the committee after the tragic events of 9/11 and was created into H.Res. 308 and passed as a "sense resolution" on December 18, 2001. We have since had it passed by the New York State Senate and Assembly as well.

The importance of National Motivation & Inspiration Day©, which is every January 2nd, is an attempt to move people from "lives of quiet desperation," to lives that have direction and purpose. Being "motivated and inspired" are only catch phrases for a deeper meaning. If you or anyone else you know literally says, "same shit different day," stop and ask yourself, "is that how I want to live my life?" Living day after day with nothing new…no new intent or direction? Like a rudderless boat floating through the sea of life and not having any sense of definitive direction or purpose? Just aimlessly floating… is that life?

"Are you a wondering generality or a meaningful specific."
~ Zig Ziglar ~

I believe that this type of mentality, which starts in the home and is reinforced throughout our lives in school and other places, leads to young adults and adults with lives that flow from one year to the next without one significant goal or objective. No written plan or strategy, just one year and then the next and then the next until one day, 5 or 10 years have passed and there is nothing to show for your life. Maybe have gained 15 or 20 pounds or worse and you're stuck in the same job with no ambition of upward mobility, just holding on for desperation to your life as it is, not the way it could be.

This concern or focus has lead me to not only create National Motivation & Inspiration Day©, but The American Motivation Awards©, Motivate America, Inc and now, potentially, the most significant addition to *"Maslow's Hierarchy of Needs"* in 60 years. I have been told that it is simply a "taxonomy" of Maslow, when in fact it is a unique and developed enhancement. It would be like saying the Maserati sports car is only a copy or advancement of the Model T, as opposed to an evolution.

Dr. Maslow's work in behavioral psychology and the establishment of his *"Hierarchy of Needs"* has had significant impact since its creation in 1953. His studies and discussions on "motivation" have impacted many areas of study, such as management, leadership, sales, marketing, education, teaching, learning, parenting, as well as the study of behavior and psychology.

I have created the *"21st Century Multidimensional Hierarchy of Needs"* in the hope that it will reignite critical discussions at companies, organizations, schools, universities and in homes to help people find balance in life while focusing on "becoming the very best U that U can be." And, of course, mentoring and helping our children to become the best that they can be.

The 21st Century Multidimensional Hierarchy of Needs Pyramid.

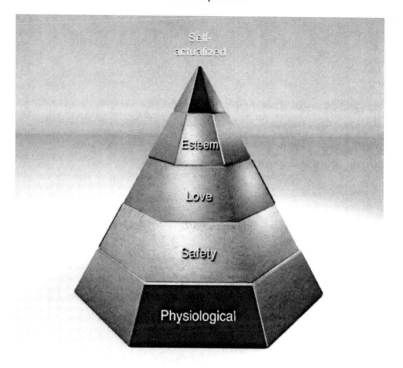

1

The 21ˢᵗ Century Multidimensional Hierarchy of Needs

In 1943, Dr. Abraham Maslow wrote the article **"A Theory of Human Motivation"**. In his article, Dr. Maslow established a theory of a needs-based human motivation. Today's MBA students, executives, managers and leaders study this theory of motivation to maximize employee and workforce management and increase "motivation" in order to increase productivity.

Since 1954 there have been many illustrations and drawings of Maslow's Hierarchy, however, the fundamental reasoning and components have always stayed the same. The basis of Maslow's theory is that human beings are motivated by <u>unsatisfied needs</u>, and that lower "needs" must be satisfied before higher needs can be satisfied. According to Maslow, there are general types of needs (physiological, survival, safety, love, and esteem) that must be satisfied before a person can move toward "self- actualization" and reaching their full-potential.

Here is the typical visual example of **"Maslow's Hierarchy of Needs"**.

Through my experiences in the fields of personal development, training, management, leadership and even marketing and advertising, Maslow's model has had a variety of uses, but still caused me to ask the simple question, "how can a one-dimensional model work in a Multidimensional world?" Most discussions and visualizations of Maslow's Hierarchy are as a one-dimensional triangle with a description of each "level," which we now understand need to be "satisfied," before a person can successfully go to the "next level" toward personal fulfillment or "self-actualization."

So. When I think of the phrase, "self-actualization," I cannot think of any other description than "how do you become the very best U that U can be?" How do you become "self-actualized" or reach "personal fulfillment?" or as the US Army's old advertising campaign used to say, "be all you can be!"

My challenge with Maslow's conclusion and model is that our world and our lives are not one dimensional and the model doesn't take this into consideration. In addition, according to the model and the stepping stones from one level to the next, one level must be satisfied, before you can successfully move to the next level, however, that seems inaccurate as well.

Even, Dr. Clay Alderfer's ERG Theory, which adds regression and progression to Maslow's Hierarchy, still did not look at it in a "multidimensional" form.

Therefore, one of the critically important theories from this book about U is for me to explain the expansion of Maslow's Hierarchy of Needs as a "one dimensional model" to the "*21st Century Multidimensional Hierarchy of Needs*" and the application of such a model in your life. How does this impact you as a person and your personal development?

Here is an example: Let's make a generalization about an 18 year old athlete in excellent physical condition, attending High School:

How many of us know or have met an 18 year old athlete in High School who might be the perfect physical specimen. He/she could not possibly achieve a higher level of peak conditioning or strength. Truly, self-fulfilled or self-actualized as a physical being… and yet, is a mediocre student, financially broke and morally corrupt. Where would this young adult fall under Maslow's model? Would they only be equal to their lowest level of accomplishment or satisfaction? Also, what happens to that very same young adult when they are in their mid-20's to 30's? When they are no longer in peak physical condition? There must be a regression or step back from their previous level of self-actualization to lower levels, right?

For this example we are only looking at four component's of a generalized and fictitious 18 year old male's life; Physical, School, Financial and Moral. What other elements help make up an average 18 year old's life?

• Physical Being
• Mental State

- Emotional State
- School or Work or Both
- Finances
- Relationships
  (parents, siblings, friends)
- Sexuality
- Faith or Religion

So, it's easy to see that while we are focusing on a four-sided pyramid, the reality is that the "average" 18 year old could have an 8-sided pyramid, depending upon the complexity of their lives and what we choose to measure or focus on. Once again, in this example we break down the components of the 18 year-old's life, to possibly determine what are the influencers in the four categories we chose to review: Physical Being; Education; Personal Finances and "Faith" / Religion, which could also be labeled, "morality" or even "social awareness and responsibility."

What are the most significant influencers upon this child's life or belief system? Answer is Nature and Nurture.

This 18 year old child is an accumulation of their genetics and lifetime experiences.

Again, I do not have the expertise it requires to break down genetic code and determine what characteristics are indeed genetic, but like most parents, when I see a child standing near their parents, I can see the resemblance. When we spend a little time together, I can see the gestures, phraseology and behaviors that are similar to their parents. Are those nature or nurture?

The point I am making for U reading this book, is that it doesn't matter, because, regardless if it's nature or nurture, in the end, it's U. And it is incumbent upon you, whether you are an 18-year old athlete in the best shape of your life or a 50 year old woman looking for happiness. Each of us, at some point in our lives must make a decision about who we are, who we want to be and how we want to live!

> *"To be, or not to be, that is the question."*
> *Shakespeare's Romeo & Juliet*

Once you have determined, *"to be"* then wouldn't it seem fitting to determine, *how to be* or *what to be*? Whether you have genetic strengths that you are enhancing in this life or you have learned a series of skills and talents that are enhancing your life, it doesn't matter. "To thyne own self be true." The Shakespearean line from Hamlet rings true. Be true to yourself. Find out who you are and what makes you happy. One of the lines I always tell interns and young adults, "Do what you love and the money will follow!"

> *"When you do what you love, you never work*
> *a day in your life."*

While these quotes and comments may seem corny or simplistic, the reality is that they are all based on truth. It seems that only in adulthood do we find these sayings to be true and thus the reason for this book! How do we change this paradigm? For years people have said, "Youth is wasted on the young." Well, if we are to evolve as a species and create new realities, at some point in time, we must find a better understanding of ourselves and a better way of communicating it to our youth. To just accept this "truth" as something we cannot change is a cop out and a failure.

2

Motivation vs. Inspiration

"I am convinced that life is 10% what happens
to me, and 90% how I react to it."
~Charles Swindoll ~

While we have laid some of the ground work for U to begin this journey of self-exploration and personal development, I need to address a very simple idea that makes this entire thing work or not work.

Many people use *motivation* and *inspiration* together as though they were interchangeable, when in fact they are quite different and complimentary and I believe, in fact, that one precedes the other. I believe that you are "inspired" first, which drives your "motivation", and gives it cause and purpose. It's kind of like a mathematical equation.

**Consciousness/Awareness >
"Inspiration"/"The Magic!" + "Motivation" >
Activity = <u>ACTION!</u>**

**And what does ACTION create ?
RESULTS! And what are "results?"**

Well, "results" can be positive or negative. We do not always get the results we intend based on the energy or dedication we put into things in our life, sometimes it doesn't work out at all… and sometimes we get negative results from our efforts. They are still results! It's just a matter of what we do with them.

In creating National Motivation & Inspiration Day©, I introduce the idea that if we start off every year with a new set of goals, that it is impossible for one year to flow into the next year without some kind of measureable change, because you must look at your own life like a company or corporation. Professional people do this all the time, but they don't do it for their own lives. Every year, companies establish goals. These goals are established as part of either an actual Business Plan or a set of 3 to 5 year goals that are intended to lead a company to *success* or successfully achieving the goals that have been set out or exceeding them.

As a manager or salesperson or production person in an assembly line, you are handed down a set of goals that if successfully accomplished will lead to your success, but also the overall success of the company. Hopefully. You know that every activity you take during a work day is in direct correlation with your overall performance and whether you are meeting, exceeding or falling behind your expected production. That production, magnified by as many other people that are doing the same activity produces a measureable output that your manager can report up to the next level.

At the secondary Manager's level, where they may have several managers reporting to them, they piece together the numbers and determine if production either meets, exceeds or falls behind the standards and expectations given to them. It is intended to work in a seamless process that eventually culminates with a completed product or service that exceeds expectations thus keeping everyone employed and being happy about the success of their team and organization.

> *"...for every action there is an equal and*
> *opposite reaction."*
>
> *~ Sir Isaac Newton ~*

Success / Achievement Chart

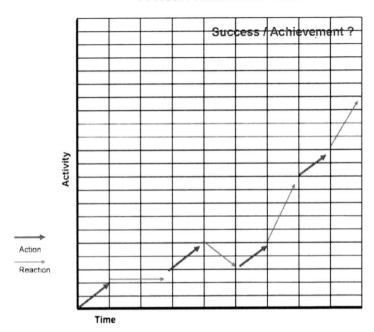

In this simplified chart above, there is a simple diagram of *action* and *reaction*. The green arrows represent an action and the red arrows indicate a reaction or result, as I referred to earlier. Regardless if it is for your professional life or your personal life, every action you take has some level of response or reaction, whether it be planned, calculated or miscalculated. Sometimes our actions create the opposite reaction that we had hoped for. Like the saying, "the road to hell is paved with good intentions." Sometimes we do things with the very best of intentions and we are absolutely bewildered and stunned by the outcome, because it isn't close to what we had intended. And, sometimes, negative results from one of our actions actually provides a better outcome in the end.

Unfortunately, for many of us, this is where we lose faith or understanding and do not appreciate why we are being tested or "building character." We cannot always guarantee that the efforts we put in place on our own behalf or for someone else or for a company will work out the way we have intended. This is where we must not lose faith in ourselves or our self-esteem. This is where the greatest challenges are in our lives and where we can find the greatest growth if we are willing to learn.

"God's delays are not God's denials."

Nobody ever said the human experience was an easy one. We are all on a journey of self.

I had a brilliant man once tell me that life is simple and people are simple if you will remember that *"people will act in their own self-interest."* In other words, people look out for themselves or do things that are in line with their own self-worth or self-belief. This is where motivation, inspiration, application and National Motivation & Inspiration Day© come together.

If we can *inspire* enough people that are willing to *ignite a flame* within themselves and those around them and direct their motivation, energy and passion toward the achievement of worthwhile goals every year, then on January 2nd of every year, National Motivation & Inspiration Day, we will not just be celebrating and recovering from New Year's Day, but rather creating an accountability for ourselves and providing direction to our lives. Not living "lives of quiet desperation" and not "same shit different day," but fulfilling lives with direction and purpose. Isn't that the way it should be?

Take Action to Make Things Happen!

So what? What does all this mean to you? I understand completely.

This book isn't about me, it's about U!

It's about you finding the "magic" in your life and the spark that will help you reach as far as you desire and reach levels of success that you never thought possible…and that doesn't mean just financial success.

What I believe Dr. Abraham Maslow originally referred to in "Maslow's Hierarchy of Needs" as achieving *self-actualization* is becoming the very best person you can become. "The best U that U can be." How can this happen without a concerted, conscious effort to do so, to be so?

You must take some form of action in order to make this happen. If you want to run a mile in 7:00 minutes, you have to run to determine if you can achieve that goal or not. If you don't the first time, do you give up or say, OK this is going to take some work. People that are good at what they do usually have some form of passion about it and work at being good at it. This is where we come back to that "nature vs. nurture" stuff again.

Think of something you are currently really proud of in your life that you have accomplished or are really good at…did you have to work at it?

The response to that question is typically, *yes* and while the results may vary, without action and activity there are very few results. Even if you choose to be a *"couch potato"* then there are results associated with that as well. So I will qualify by saying, there are very few <u>positive</u> things that happen in this world without positive action toward a specific goal. The easier way of describing it is simply, **"stimulus > response."**

As I have stated, motivation and inspiration are two different things, however, used together very frequently.

So let's discuss "*Inspiration*" first, because that is where I think it starts. Michelangelo, Benjamin Franklin, Thomas Edison or Henry Ford had to have been inspired through their imagination or creativity to create the things that they created.

> "...*your dreams are life's coming attractions.*"
> ~ *Albert Einstein* ~

There are several definitions used to describe "*inspiration*," and I like these:

- A divine influence directly and immediately exerted upon the mind or soul.
- The divine quality of the writings or words of a person so influenced.
- Stimulation of the mind or emotions to a high level of feeling or activity.
- The condition of being so stimulated.

As I said, I like these descriptions, however, to enhance the point I would make the analogy that inspiration is like...a match! A flash! A spark! Something that ignites. Ignites fire, Ignites gasoline, ignites an idea, your imagination and ignites people!

We often look at other people as being "inspirational," however, when was the last time you were inspired? What did it feel like?

Quick .... What are the 5 things you feel when you are inspired? What happens that very moment?

1. _____
2. _____
3. _____
4. _____
5. _____

I'm sure you wrote things like; butterflies, nervous, excited, thrilled, enthusiastic, and energetic. These are great descriptions of feeling inspired. But then what? What happens next?

This is one of the most tragic things that happen to young adults and people in general. Many become uncertain, scared, self-conscious, embarrassed and in the worst cases afraid. … Afraid to act, afraid to fail even afraid to move. Think about how opposite those feelings are:

- Butterflies   > Afraid
- Nervous   > Uncertain
- Excited   > Scared
- Thrilled   > Self Conscious
- Enthusiastic   > Embarrassed
- Energetic   > Fearful

Some young adults have those feelings of insecurity instilled at an early age. They learn not to trust themselves; or be uncertain; be scared and then of course be self-conscious on top of all of that. Once reinforced long enough with comments like; "you're stupid," "you're fat," "you're lazy," and of course the favorite of all, "you'll never amount to anything," which I was told in High School. These types of things are said far too often too far too many children and it rips away their dignity and self-respect and courage.

The greatest lie ever told to us by our parents was that, "sticks and stones may break my bones, but words will never hurt me."

Words are the most powerful and destructive tool man has at their disposal and many times used by adults to destroy children and young adults…like a surgeon using a chain saw for a circumcision.

So, of course, as a teenager/young adult it becomes difficult to not have that negative reinforcement show itself. I have a saying that I have used for years in my sessions: the greatest lie ever told us by our parents and teachers was that "sticks and stones may break my bones, but words will never hurt me." The reality is that words are the most powerful things we possess. This is one of the most critical items to take away from this book. Words and communication are one of the most critically important skills of a successful adult. Few people think of themselves as lawyers or an editor of a paper…taking every word into consideration before using it. Most adults just explode with venom that stings and scars children, leaving them emotionally beaten and battered. When it happens often enough, a child either buys into it or believes it or rebels against it, which is a human being's natural instinct for "Fight or Flight." And, unfortunately, like abusive parents raising another generation of abusive parents… children from verbally abusive homes tend to have communication issues and become verbally abusive adults.

So, let's get back to, what inspires you?

For many young adults there is a period of being lost and uncertain. If you think of a "drug addict" or "alcoholic," they have difficulty thinking, processing information and communicating. Well, young adults have massive amounts of "chemical changes" and "hormonal changes" that make it difficult to think at times as well as be "who they are."

In this mix of chemical and hormonal influences it is difficult for many teenagers and young adults to figure themselves out and figure out what inspires or motivates them. It is also a time for changes in social structures, peer pressure and changes in interests. For instance, many young adults were great athletes when they were young. It was fun and made them happy. As teens, they lose interest and become uncertain of what they would like to do next, but they know the interest they had at a younger age does not satisfy them or make them happy or inspire them any longer. Nor do they feel motivated to compete at that level.

For young men this is very common. As sports become very competitive and boys become men, many lose their advantage and fall behind. Many young men are uncertain of what to become if they are not athletes or "*jocks*." This is becoming more prominent with young women as well, because of the advancement of women's sports. As young, prepubescent girls they were great athletes ("Tom Boys"), but once their body changes, that is it, especially in sports like gymnastics. No more interest in sports for their bodies have changed the way they feel about running around or how well they performed. They become too self-conscious and quit.

There are groups of teens and young adults, however that are very fortunate. They know from a young age what they want to be or do. They know what they enjoy and are driven toward success. For many of them there is a different challenge of not pushing too hard and being too hard on themselves. They also typically have family pressure to perform, which also has a variety of outcomes, positive and negative.

So, we still need to address, *what inspires you*? This takes time to consider and I will provide you with some questions that may help bring this top of mind for you.

Let's stick with our example, if you enjoyed being an athlete… what was it that you enjoyed? The competition? The team work? The comradery? It is important to isolate what made it so much fun. This may be a key to help you determine, "what you want to be when you grow up."

Can you provide yourself a quick list of 5 things that you really enjoy doing?

GO !

1. _____

2. _____

3. _____

4. _____

5. _____

OK. If you couldn't come up with any or you decided not to participate, here is another shot at it, but let's do it a little differently.

Please, sit comfortably in your chair. Sit all the way back, not slouched over or laying back. Sit at attention. Close your eyes and take a really deep breath. Cleanse your mind of all thoughts…take another deep breath.

Think of something in your past that you truly enjoyed doing. Put yourself in that place it is NOT with someone else…just yourself…what did you enjoy and why. Concentrate on the joy, the feelings of being content and happy.

Take the time to really feel the happiness and experience the emotions of joy.

Here is an example:

When I think of *playing soccer…*

It makes me feel 1) happy inside

2) energized by the exercise

3) having fun with others and being a part of something

4) trying to win and achieve

5) fighting to be the best I can be…

OK. So your turn to finish the following sentence:

When I think of doing _____ ...

It makes me feel   1) _____

2) _____

3) _____

4) _____

5) _____

Now, the challenge becomes making connections. In my case of enjoying soccer, you might come to the conclusion of, well dummy, keep playing soccer. That's not where I want you to go, it's what other things can you do that can make you have the same feelings?

If I am trying to find a career or something that makes me happy, but "playing soccer" (or whatever it might be) is not a possibility right now... what are other things I can do to duplicate the positive feelings I had playing soccer:

1) happy inside
2) energized by the exercise
3) having fun with others and being a part of something
4) trying to win and achieve
5) fighting to be the best I can be...

Combining the list, what "exercise" oriented thing can I do that provides "fun with others" and being "a part of something" to try and "win and achieve" and "be the best I can be"....

What are things I can consider being or doing:

• being a coach
• being a counselor
• being a teacher or educator

- a sports team physical therapist
- a camp counselor for the summer

So, in my search for being inspired I found a few things that could possibly make me happy. Being happy about what I do can help achieve higher levels of success and a personal sense of fulfillment.

"Do what you love and the money will follow."

Our challenge in most of America is that we compare that level of *fulfillment* with the amount of money we make and where we live and what we drive. In many countries around the world you might measure success by the amount of children and happiness you have in your life. Your level of contentment, not the amount of money. In recent years, we have great examples of people / celebrities that have all the money they could want and yet lived terribly closed off and isolated lives. Anna Nicole Smith and Michael Jackson are just two examples of people that "had it all," but were living pretty miserable lives.

I heard a great story once to illustrate this point:

There was a young man from New York City on a business trip in western Mexico on the Pacific Ocean. The young man watched this older local man during his stay that had wonderful widgets for sale that were hand made. Some days the gentleman would be taking a siesta. Other days he would be playing with his children and singing to his wife.

So, one day the young man from New York introduced himself and told this gentleman that he could be very wealthy from these amazing widgets. The Mexican gentleman said, Si senior, please tell me more. With that, the man from New York told him that he could take these widgets to New York and sell thousands of them. As a matter of fact, we could go public and sell millions of them !

The Mexican gentleman exclaimed, ay carumba ! What else do we need to do senior? Tell me more!

The young man went on to describe the millions of dollars and the IPO and all the wonders of being rich !

The Mexican gentleman had another simple question for this young New Yorker….so then what senior, then what?

Well, that's the best part, you get to sell all your shares and live where ever you want, even on the Pacific and enjoy peaceful days and nights in your retirement.

The Mexican gentleman said with a smile…senior, I already have this? Why would I go through all of that trouble and all of that aggravation when I already live in a beautiful community near the ocean with my beautiful wife and children. I have enough money and the love of my family and friends.

The young man from New York seemed perplexed and thought the Mexican gentleman did not understand. After his long journey home with many delays and travel issues, he got home to his own family and enjoyed a beautiful summer day in Central Park walking with his beautiful wife and playing with his adoring children…and as he laid in The Great Meadow looking at all of the people with a backdrop of the New York skyline, it hit him.

No matter what he did in life or where he traveled or how much money he made, he could never replace the simplicity and love of being with his wife and children in the place he called, home.

What is the moral to the story? Well, I hope you see it for yourself, however, I think it simply means to enjoy and appreciate what you have. When you live in the now and enjoy the actual beauty of what you have, opposed to what you don't have, you will enjoy your life that much more.

*"It's not having what you want, but wanting
what you have…"*
~ Cheryl Crow ~

I recently stated at a High School Career Day an outlandish statement that just happens to also be true. I said, "Mother Theresa was selfish!" How in the world could I make a ridiculous comment like that? One of the most unselfish and giving human beings this planet has ever known.

Simple. If there was not a sense of fulfillment, accomplishment or possibly serving her need to give and serve others she would probably not have been able to sustain and give to the level in which she did. Therefore, there was a sense of personal satisfaction and serving herself through serving others.

What's the purpose here? Well, it's two-fold. Most people have heard the phrase, "do what you love and the money will follow." Well, this is absolutely true for many reasons.

First and foremost, when you do what you love, it brings joy and happiness into your life. One of the greatest tragedies I see with adults is that they feel "stuck." Stuck doing things they hate to do. Feeling the pressure of continuing a job or career that brings them no joy. Please realize that this is a choice…and it is one that occurs at an earlier age. When you choose not to continue your education, you are also choosing to limit your career choices. So, it is unfair to beat yourself up later or be mad about the career choices you have without a college degree or advanced degree. However, there are many people that have been very successful without a college degree. I personally know several CEOs of companies that never attended college. These are few and far between, but it can be done. There are also many vocations, such as electrician, or plumber or carpenter that do not require a college degree and yet you can make a very nice living and raise your family well. Jesus was the son of a carpenter and he did OK.

All these stories are well and good, but what does this mean to U?

Well, it's about making the right choices for the right reasons. As young adults, I have seen way too many make choices based on "peer pressure" or what one friend or another is doing. While friends are certainly important you know there is no way for me to get past the great line that every parent has said at one point or other, "If your friend (Johnny) jumps off the bridge, are you going to jump off the bridge?" This is where we begin to get into the questions I asked about our advancement and why we still face the same challenges we did centuries ago. It also begins to bridge into Psychology and behavior.

I am not a Psychologist or Psychiatrist. This book is not intended to provide you psychological guidance nor am I suggesting it takes the place of therapy.

What I am stating though, is that you can spend your life complaining and pointing at others and blaming them for your lot in life or you can get focused, get inspired, get motivated and create a plan of action to live the life that you want. Your behaviors and actions will be what you live without excuses. You will be able to look at your life as something you are actively engaged in and the "captain of your own ship" or you can be a bystander in your own life story and tell people, "same shit, different day."

Welcome to the "Human Experience" ~ it's your choice !

3

U! What Makes up You and Your Life?

I believe that Dr. Abraham Maslow and his "Hierarchy of Needs" is very accurate as it pertains to a person's development and the desire to "advance" and "satisfy" various "needs" before obtaining a sense of love/belonging, self-esteem and ultimately "self-actualization," however, I believe that it is Multidimensional in nature, not one dimensional, as his model is typically shown.

Maslow's Hierarchy of Needs	21st Century Multidimensional Hierarchy of Needs

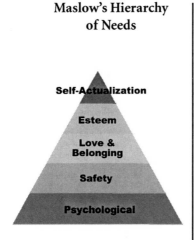

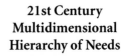

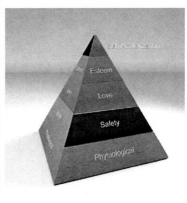

For those who are not familiar with Dr. Maslow and Maslow's *"Hierarchy of Needs."* You must first understand that you move up the scale as you satisfy each level. Therefore, you cannot be successful at Relationships in Love/Belonging unless you are secure in the areas of Physiological and Safety. So, you cannot be successful in achieving *"self-actualization"* or becoming *"self-fulfilled"* unless each of the other components is satisfied and secure.

However, I believe that there is another level of complexity. Human behavior and the Human Experience are Multidimensional, just like the human genome, not one dimensional like Maslow's original model. And as Dr. Clay Alderfer's ERG Theory also suggests that there is progression and regression within the hierarchy itself. As you reach certain levels or milestones in your life you may be at one level of "satisfaction," but then regress as you evolve or mature.

So, you see that the diagram is much the same, however, now it is a true pyramid and you can be at different levels on each side of the pyramid, which now leaves room for people that are struggling in some aspects of their life, but striving in other areas. It allows for people that are excelling in their work environment, but a nightmare in their home environment and vice versa. Although, I am sure that Dr. Maslow considered people as a whole unit and regardless of where they were that they would be themselves. Kind of like that joke, "no matter where you go in the world, there you are." No matter where you go in this world, you can't get away from "yourself." This is part of our lifelong journey.

In order to get a better understanding of the advancement or "satisfaction" of each level we need to determine what would be considered successfully, satisfying that need, before you can advance to the next level of the Hierarchy.

I also think it is important to recognize that from the earliest stages of development all the way to our death, we go through the 5 stages presented by Dr. Maslow every time we change an environment. A new home, a new job, a new relationship or a new location. Every time we make a change, we must satisfy these needs in order to be fulfilled, self-actualized or be the best we can be. It may happen at a faster pace or once we understand ourselves better and are potentially more mature or more "evolved," there is less time or effort asserted in each of the stages, because we understand how to meet and satisfy each need or level.

Let's look at what might be required to "satisfy" each level:

Physiological Needs, Maslow considered such things as; breathing; food; water; sex; sleep; homeostasis and excretion.

Basic bodily human functions. Without successfully "satisfying" these fundamental needs for existence, it is

impossible to look beyond this toward safety or belonging or esteem, because your fundamental needs as a human being are not being met.

Look at some of the most impoverished places on the planet, like Haiti, Africa or Pakistan. Even in the best of times things are difficult, but when there is a natural disaster their entire lives are swept away. The very fundamental battle for sustenance and existence takes over. There are few rules and the physical world takes over…Darwinism takes over. Brutality and harshness reign.

Therefore, in places around the world, which include parts of the United States, where actual physiological needs cannot be taken for granted and existence is literally fought for every day, it is impossible to advance to a level of "Safety" or security.

Safety Needs are listed as; security of body;

employment; resources; morality; family; health and property. This level is essentially self-explanatory. Once you have created an environment where you are physiologically meeting your basic needs, you then need to have a sense of security or safety. As "pack animals," this is typically gained by feeling secure in a group or pack where we are not alone facing danger. In modern western language it would be the ability to feel safe coming and going from your home. Feeling secure that your home and your belongings are safe and that you will face no physical harm.

If you think of the nightly news in America or reading your daily newspaper, much of our country struggles to pass this level. There are many communities that are not safe. People live in constant fear that they will be hurt or their things will be stolen. Much like prey from a pack of wolves. Leaving your den or dwelling, leaves an impending sense of insecurity whether you will be attacked or not?

In recent years, after the terrorist attack of 9/11 there has been a new focus on security and safety. People did not feel safe at their place of business. There was uncertainty whether you could be hurt coming or going from your home or office. Once again, the physical world takes over. The threat of violence that some-how equalizes any work that has been done to create esteem or belonging can be destroyed when your sense of security and safety is taken away. Ask any victim of a violent crime.

One of the greatest fears caused by the terrorist attacks of 9/11 is whether The United States of America would be turned into a "third world country," into a primitive country if "Wall Street" collapsed or if its electrical supply was elimi-nated? Well, would we? Since the attacks of 9/11 our world and our country has changed and may never be the same. In essence, the terrorists won. We have to wait in ridiculous lines to get through security. Our financial system has been in disarray ever since.

The global economy has been shaken. Nothing has been the same since those terrorist attacks.

In essence, the terrorist acts of 9/11 in some ways put the entire world on this plane of existence where we cannot securely get beyond a fundamental level of "safety" or security in order to advance toward "World Peace" or global acceptance and mass "self-actualization."

If we look at these communities and societies that live their lives in this fashion of killing and intimidation, where they encourage people to give their own lives as a symbol of "accomplishment," where they treat women and children as property, they are literally stuck at this level of "safety needs" and it is impossible to evolve. And they intentionally are trapped there for many reasons as a culture, but certainly one of the most important reasons is because they have connected it to a faith, religion and belief system. If you do not believe what they believe, then you must be killed.

I know of no surer way to eliminate growth and evolution of man than to kill all those that do not believe in your own self-limiting belief system. It would be like one of the gangs in America taking over and if you did not believe the same exact things they did and conducted yourself in the same criminal mentality, that you would be killed. Literally turning back our culture hundreds of years.

Writing this as an American, with my viewpoint of the world and the "human experience," I must admit that I can say I have a biased view of the world. As much as I would like to say that the "human experience" is the same for everyone that is born, that would be incorrect. Once again, we come back to "Nature vs. Nurture." The "natural state" of being born and having the genetic code of your parents cannot be argued, but depending upon the environment and the level of existence that you are born into, your existence and "nurture" can change from the moment you are born. Whether it be in a war-torn country or the deprivation and poverty of a third-world country, from the moment you are born you are being developed and if it be the threat of death from violence or famine, it becomes a part of your genetic makeup of who you are.

If you look on a personal and local level, opposed to a global level, then you certainly have individuals that move beyond the level of "safety / security" to the next level of "Love and Belonging," but I believe there are significant nuances to these levels. The first two levels of the Hierarchy are relatively simple and self-explanatory, while the next three levels become more complex and nuanced. This is also where I believe "progression, regression" and "bullying" come into play.

In "**Love and Belonging**" Maslow refers to: friends, family and sexual intimacy. Once again, this is self-explanatory in some ways, but more far reaching than most people realize and taken for granted. While dealing with a majority of people, one can say that you are born into a loving family, however, this is not true for everyone.

Being a part of a "loving family," would also assume that there are friends and loved ones around that share love and kindness with each other and our children. This is yet another stage where we must take a closer look at "nature vs. nurture."

I love listening to Dr. Deepak Chopra speak about "bliss." He makes it sound so extraordinary and something I hope more and more people find at some point in their lives. When a "healthy" child is born with all its "pure potentiality" in place and once again, hopefully we are dealing with a majority of children born, every interaction provides some stimulus and some response. It provides some mark or imprint on our lives, whether it be positive, negative or neutral.

For most children in the world, how is "love" expressed? A smile. A hug. A kiss. Laughter and joy. If this were the foundation of every child ever born, what do you think the world would be like? If every child knew true love, dedication and "unconditional love" and a life filled with happiness and joy from parents, friends and family how wonderful would this world be?

Unfortunately, that is not the case. Many children are born into poverty. Poverty of mind, body and spirit. Regardless how you look upon the birth of a child, it is truly a miracle, but it is also the most natural of things that we do. We forget, just like most animals, mothers give birth to children every minute of every day all around the world. In the wild, "babies" are born in all sorts of circumstances. Many die at birth. Many are killed at birth. Many starve to death and never make it through their first days. Regrettably, the birth of a human baby isn't much different.

There are many places around the world where a child that is born is unwelcome. It does not bring joy or happiness, but rather sadness and in some cases shame and anger. We see too often right here in America where newborns are left to die or unattended. We have abortions and killing of babies. So, when we speak of "Love and belonging" we must realize that these truths do exist and do influence our view of the world and our own interactions with friends, family and loved ones.

Staying once again with the majority of children, especially those in America, we can assume that they are born into this world and cherished by parents, family and friends. They are nurtured and given the most luxurious of shelters in the world, fed and educated. Once in the school system, those that conform and fit into our educational model are treated well by teachers and encouraged to learn and grow. For those that may be more active or "tactile" learners, our traditional educational systems do not handle them well and those children are given various routes of education and in some instances, medicated to conform so they are not a distraction in the classroom, which will come back to haunt us at some time in the future. Statistically, these tend to be more boys than girls.

The stage of "Love and Belonging" is broad, because it covers a wide array of life experiences from newborns to school age to those near death. Having a sense of "belonging" and being loved by others sets the stage for life or helps someone pass into the next life knowing they were loved and a part of something greater than themselves.

Again, I think the concept for an adult to have a sense of "love and belonging" they must understand what that means. It means regardless of whether you are a multimillionaire living in a secluded resort community or a drug addicted prostitute, if you are embraced by the people around you, then you have a sense of "love and belonging" regardless of how fleeting or truly pathetic or insecure. As a human being it meets that need of "love and belonging."

Unfortunately, this is also the foundation of "bullying" and "bigotry." As "pack animals" we tend to be attracted to others that are like us in some way. Just like Elephants stay with elephants and monkeys hang out with other monkeys. The human species are "pack animals" that connect on a variety of levels, but are certainly drawn together based on commonalities.

Once again drawing into our cross hairs the discussion of evolution. Why do we still have difficulty accepting those that are different? Whether it be the way they look or a behavior we do not understand, we tend to reject those that do not "fit in." I think this is most obviously seen in the behavior of children and teenagers. They are not mature enough yet to understand why they feel the way they feel, but there is a strong desire to form "cliques" and push away those that do not "fit in.

Many of these barriers border around race, socio-economics and sexual preference. This would also be the foundation for "Bigotry," which is defined as:

1. stubborn and complete intolerance of any creed, belief, or opinion that differs from one's own.
2. the actions, beliefs, prejudices, etc., of a bigot.

—Synonyms

1. narrow-mindedness, bias, discrimination.

In recent news there have been several stories of young men that were or presumed to be "gay" and committed suicide. One young man was attacked by a group of other boys and the other was a college student that was "outed" on Facebook having a sexual encounter with another male college student. I first suggest that we be careful what we label "bullying" and not associate that with what is criminal.

In the first case, where the young man was attacked by three other young men is called "assault." That is not "bullying." In many states that is also considered a "hate crime."

In the second case of videotaping a young man having sex with another man and then putting it out on the Internet, there are a variety of laws that were broken.

Therefore, I suggest that we make sure we do not "over use" the phrase "bullying" to include activities that are actually criminal in nature and we have laws already in place to prosecute people that break the law.

"Bullying" or the use of words or intimidation to influence others is different. It's abusive and mean spirited. There are millions of children that are "bullied" or teased by other children for a variety of reasons, because they are: short, tall, skinny, fat, "ugly," stupid, smart, black, white, gay and a variety of other reasons why one group will pick on another group or individuals. We must first understand that it is a basic human behavior to differentiate oneself from others and have a sense of belonging with a group, "pack" or "clique." If we are truly trying to "evolve," then we must begin to discuss how we teach our children "acceptance" of others and tolerance of behavior that they do not understand and even what they do not like.

This is where much of the difficulty exists.

It may be easy to accept someone that you have little interaction with or has behavior that is "offensive." If there is a minority or a specific group of people that feel that they are being discriminated against and I have a "bad interaction" with someone that is either Black or Jewish, for example, and I say that I really don't like that person because they are a "jerk," I am entitled to that opinion, am I not? Or do I immediately become an "Anti-Semite" or "racist?"

That is significantly different then expecting the "human species" to accept something that is seen as harmful, disruptive and threatening.

Earlier in the book, I used the terrorist attacks of 9/11 as an example. There were a group of men that happened to be "Muslim" and from the "Middle East." Their pictures and background are very well documented. This is not an assumption, but based in fact. The "average American" does not have "Muslim" friends nor have they attended services in a Mosque. So much of what they are learning comes from the media and nightly news or daily newspapers. They know that these men that are now referred to as "terrorists" lived here in the United States, attended and met at Mosques and prayed. They also plotted under our noses and carried out these terrible acts.

Why then, would the Muslim community be upset or mad at Americans for not trusting them? At this level of "love, belonging" and next "esteem," you can see why there may be a sense of uncertainty. Yes, there are generalizations that have been made, but unfortunately it is based on our lower level of security and need for safety that we make these assumptions.

What people are arguing is for human beings to not use their senses and judgment to come to reasonable conclusions. There were a group of terrorists that flew planes into the World Trade Center and Pentagon killing thousands of Americans. There were pictures indicating who they were and they all looked very similar…of Middle Eastern dissent. So, are you wrong for being cautious or worried about other similar looking people?

This scenario happens to also be true for several other minority groups and the "generalizations" and judgments that are made about them, as there have been for the generations of immigrants that came to America before them. Just ask the Irish and Italians. Yes, it is unfair. And yes, the world would be a better place if we were less judgmental and made fewer generalizations about people. However, here is a little test for you:

Over the next several nights, watch your nightly news, both local and national and read a national newspaper and then answer these questions:

1. What race are "terrorists," generally? _____
2. What race is a typical "gang member?" _____

3. What race is a "white collared criminal?" _____
4. What race most commonly commits murder? _____
5. What race gets in the most car accidents? _____
6. What race most commonly gets DWI's? _____

So, there is a little exercise that you can do all by yourself. Do you find the answers interesting? Are they true? Is your "perception" accurate or is the information and visual data that you have taken in over a week's period statistically inaccurate?

This exercise is meant to reinforce that we all make assumptions based on the information that we take in and is in no way intended to reinforce stereotypes, but they do happen for a reason. Why? Referring back to the communities that value suicide or killing others in the name of God or other spiritual leader. If a child is born into that environment and raised by a loving family and community that stick to this value or belief system, they are more than likely going to embrace this belief system as well, because of this sense of "love and belonging." It may not seem right to the rest of the world, but in order to fit into that community in which they are raised and reach this level of "love and belonging" they must embrace this belief system or be rejected or killed.

The beauty of "pack animals" and the human experience is that regardless of when or where or how you grew up, there is a sense of belonging or connectivity to your roots. The people that connected with you at a young age, your family and friends, your neighborhood. "Brooklyn in the house!," I hear people say. I have never understood it, but young and old, people from Brooklyn, NY have a sense of pride and belonging when the name "Brooklyn" is announced.

Regardless of upbringing this is an important part of every human being. Some people respond negatively to the mention of their hometown or their neighborhood. Why? Some people hope to *evolve* beyond their neighborhood or what they were born into. The sense of *upward mobility* or moving up a class in order to have more riches or belongings is one of the strongest motivators I know.

The next piece of the hierarchy is complicated. Sexual intimacy. If you notice, "sex" is used as one of the "physiological" and fundamental needs of a human being. Like most animals, our sexuality and sexual drive is largely driven by the need to procreate. Finding a mate as a human being is part of our journey.

I remember once in High School, I went to a Catholic High School, during Senior year in an Impromptu Speaking Class the teacher decided that he would try to embarrass me and asked me to speak about "Sex" to the classroom. At 6' 3" and barely 160 lbs., I had just gone through puberty myself and had very little experience with "sex," in the way most people think of it, so, I began a conversation that I think still rings true today. Instead of speaking about the act or the urge of "sex," I spoke about the "transformation" of sexuality. That all of us at that time were young men and women that had just gone through changes and were curious about our own sexuality and dealing with the insecurity of our bodies changing, acne and confusion.

All I remember is the teacher staring at me in amazement and giving me a thumbs up and an "A" as the classroom clapped loudly.

There are several challenges regarding 'sexual intimacy" as it pertains to "love and belonging" in Maslow's third step of personal human development. I believe there are some people that are "non sexual" in nature and there are others that "ooze" sexuality from an early age. The power of sexual intimacy on some people is overbearing even as adults.

They remain insecure and uncertain almost petrified by an encounter. Others, can't wait to be sexually active with others, never mind curious about their own sexuality.

I have heard references of children at the age of 10 and under being sexually active, whether it be through masturbation or intercourse. I find it horrifying, but they are a product of their environment. In some countries and cities, even here in the United States where children as young as 10 or younger are looking for "sexual intimacy" as a sense of *belonging* and the desire to be *loved*. Once again, the drive and the need for *belonging* can be so powerful that seeking out something that a child could have no idea what it means will do just in order to feel loved, connected or a sense of belonging.

Sadly, "sexual intimacy" is forced upon some young women and young men without their understanding or consent. The worst of these stories are in Africa where "Witch Doctors" have told grown men with AIDS – HIV that the only way for them to get rid of the AIDS –HIV virus is to have intercourse with a child / virgin. So, in Africa, there are grown men that have intercourse with infant girls in order to get rid of their AIDS – HIV, which we know is ridiculous, but they don't. What is to happen to a poor little girl that has no idea what has happened to her and is already diseased before they can even speak?

Just as sadly, in America, where you would think our education system has helped educate children to know better or even educate parents to teach our children better, unfortunately not. In poor communities around the country where teen pregnancy runs high and gangs run rampant, teenage girls and boys try to get a sense of "belonging" by fitting into gangs. As rituals to become a "member" or "belong" they are forced into sexual intimacy of the cruelest and harshest ways. Girls are forced to have group sex or "gang bangs" with groups of boys in order to "get in." Boys are given orders of how many girls they need to have "sex with," even if by force, in order to be accepted.

In these cases, whether it be in Africa or America, what are these children going to evolve into? Once these barriers have been crossed and destroyed, where do they find self-worth, self-esteem or value when it has already been taken away or they have given it away in order to fit in?

For many of you reading this now, you may think this is so foreign and bizarre based on your own personal experience, but once again, think about "belonging" and where we find comfort. Not uncommonly, we tend to find comfort with people that are "like us." Whether it be in race, creed, culture, religion or neighborhood, we as human beings and "pack animals" tend to find a sense of belonging with people that are like us.

"Don't surround yourself with yourself…"
Yes ~ Song "I've Seen All Good People"

The difficult reality is that "love and belonging" is a topic, subject and category that entire books are written about. I certainly cannot cover the entire topic in a few pages, but suffice to say that this level may be the most critical and challenging stage in the "hierarchy of needs."

The desire for most human beings to be with people that are like them…to find a sense of comfort and "belonging" is potentially responsible for our lack of advancement and evolution as a species. As we advance in many ways our human tendency and behavior is to seek comfort with what has come before. Hence, the very drive of some people to advance and change us as human beings is met with a fundamental and possibly genetic desire to fall back and find peace, comfort and belonging.

Naturally, this desire and drive for a sense of "belonging / love" once "satisfied," leads to the next level in the hierarchy, which is "Esteem."

In the stage of **"Esteem"** one must meet the need of creating "self-esteem," confidence, achievement, respect of others and respect by others.

If you followed the examples in the previous stage of Love/Belonging, the creation of "esteem," makes sense. Once you have "joined the gang" or "been on the street" or sold millions of dollars of drugs, stocks or bonds, you have potentially created "esteem."

Regardless of where you come from, as a group or "pack" of human beings, if you have "passed the test" to "belong" to a certain group, you create a personal sense of confidence, achievement and self-esteem, whether it be a false sense is irrelevant for right now. Once you have passed whatever threshold of entry there is, whether it's having sex with several partners in order to join a gang, or selling drugs to fit into another gang or selling enough ads or stocks or bonds or cars or if it's having enough money to live in a prestigious neighborhood or join a club, whatever the threshold of entry, once you have "paid the price," you can begin to find a sense of "esteem." Many successful people love to be near other "successful people." "Masters of the universe," they call them in the corporate world, people that have reached a level of "mutual respect" or "esteem" for each other based on some set of standards.

The great thing about being objective and looking at the "human experience" from a distance, is that you can see regardless of what the standards are and regardless of what, where, who or when you live, there is a sense of "love and belonging" that grows into "mutual respect" and "Esteem" from the lowest of drug dealers to multi-millionaires in the stock market, like Bernie Madoff.

In a recent "White Paper" outlining the *21ˢᵗ Century Multi-dimensional Hierarchy of Needs*, I refer to Bernie Madoff as an example. His story is one that will be studied for years to come. How a single man could swindle thousands of people out of billions of dollars is an amazing study in sociology, psychology, corruption, incompetence and stupidity. I have heard people say, "how could people be so stupid!?" Of course, they must have never been lied to by a child or a spouse. To have someone fool you and take away your money, your time, your trust and your dignity is a terrible thing. Whether Bernie Madoff would be considered a classic "sociopath" is up for discussion by those far more qualified than me, but the question I address, was how was he able to get so many people to trust him?

In this discussion of "esteem," he was able to elevate himself to a level of esteem that others, with a lot of money, held him in high esteem and regard. They actually fought to have him invest their money. What is also amazing was that he manipulated not just the financial community, but also took advantage of his faith and the Jewish Community. His ability to create a larger than life image was his pathway to manipulation and corruption. Not only corruption by legal standards, but also corruption of the mind and soul. Bernie Madoff's story is a complex one, because he knew all along that he was misleading and stealing from people and yet was so morally corrupt himself that he perpetuated the lie for years. This type of moral corruption, which we also saw with the demise of Tiger Woods are the types of deception that break people's belief and spirit. This type of moral corruption puts us as a society in the position of disbelief. Not only at how unethical and immoral these two men were, but makes us question, "who can we trust?"

When we share our esteem for people, that comes with our trust and respect. When we "esteem" someone, it typically comes over time. It takes time to show who you are and what you are made of…your "character." So, when people like a Bernie Madoff or Tiger Woods are exposed in our community, in our midst, we as a society lose. For those that have had the tragedy of infidelity, the most significant loss is that of your faith in yourself and in others. Having gone through it myself and having read books in order to recover, when a spouse or lover commits adultery or cheats, it isn't just the act of infidelity, it's what they take away from you. Very few of these situations exist without someone asking questions. If someone is in fact cheating or lying to you, at some point in time you sense it and ask questions, because your gut tells you too. So, whether it's Bernie Madoff stealing your money or it's Tiger Woods cheating on his beautiful young wife, over and over again, at some point in time they were asked if they were cheating or stealing or lying and they lied again. With each and every lie that's told a small part of your faith and trust is stolen with it, because when you entrust someone with your life and swear, 'til death do us part," or give someone your lifetime savings and they manipulate and steal it from you, it becomes hard for everyone to trust, to esteem others.

Just like mortality, it makes us question ourselves and our own commitments and relationships. If I trust someone and they have a high level of "esteem" from me…how do I know that they are not lying to me? And, if I was so naïve to believe them for so long, then there must be something wrong with me, because I couldn't see it. I didn't do anything about it. That is the most tragic loss, is your own "self-esteem" and your ability to trust yourself and your personal judgment of character, because you then feel vulnerable to do it again.

After the Bernie Madoff scam was uncovered there were several other similar "schemes" uncovered and it impacted not only Wall Street, but Main Street and anyone that invested in the markets. How do I know that I can trust these people with my money.

These two examples are obviously from recent news and great examples of "mass esteem" or community impact, but what of personal "self-esteem?" What must we do in order to increase, maximize or successfully satisfy our sense of "self-esteem?"

"Self-esteem" is an interesting thing. It is defined as, "confidence in your own merit as an individual person." Not to be confused with "ego." In today's "Reality TV" environment where everyone thinks they should be on television and far too many people that do not belong on television are, people confuse having a high "self-esteem" with having an enormous ego that is trying desperately to compensate for actually not having self-esteem.

The "Real Housewives of …where ever" or "Jersey Shore" or "Real Life" are actually the proverbial "car wrecks" that you can't take your eyes off. You're embarrassed for the person, you're mortified that anyone is actually paying attention and then you realize that they actually think they have talent or beauty and belong on television! Little do they realize that the "reality" of them being on TV is because at cocktail parties and get- togethers all around America people that can stomach watching the programs are actually laughing at them not with them. That's not "esteem."

So, the healthy development of someone to have a good sense of themselves and respect for themselves, where does that come from? When does it develop? How is it reinforced?

Here we are again, back to "Nature vs. Nurture." Someone can be born into a family of power, prestige and leadership, but that does not mean that a child in that environment will have a healthy sense of self or a healthy "self-esteem." In fact, there are many that are born into families of power that feel inferior and insecure and turn to drugs and alcohol.

A child can be born with amazing talents, but if never put in the proper place to shine or develop those talents, they may be squandered or even have an opposite effect. If a child is verbally abused throughout their childhood that they are not "good enough"…at what point do they believe it? Or, does it become the "fuel," the motivating factor, that drives someone to success to overcome?

Quickly, off the top of your head, What are 5 things you were told as a child about yourself ?

1. _____
2. _____
3. _____
4. _____
5. _____

Check the ones that had the greatest impact.

Are they true? Are they "good" or "bad?" Did they become a *self-fulfilling prophecy?*" or is it something specific to you that you cannot change?

For some people, what they were told as children about themselves is something they still believe, either positive or negative. Some people, while you are speaking to them will say the most terrible or outlandish things about themselves.

While it could be seen as being light or "self-effacing," in many cases they mean it.

"Many truths are said in jest."
~ Confucius ~

Here you have just one component of Maslow's original "Hierarchy of Needs" that volumes of books have been written on and frankly, I feel we are no closer to understanding the "cause and effect" or solution for how to make these things better for people than we were when Dr. Maslow first wrote about motivating people and his "Hierarchy of Needs" in 1943.

Finally, "*self-actualization*." To be personally fulfilled...to be "the best U that U can be."

Is this the "pinnacle" of life? What is the purpose of life? Why do we exist? What is our lifetime intended to be and what are we supposed to take away from this existence? Or, are we just like the other animals on the planet, from the Ameba to the Zebra, from the Algae to the worm, is there no greater purpose for our existence and when we die there is nothing. As some refer to it, we simply become, "plant food."

For Maslow, the highest level of personal development was to be "self-actualized" or reach "personal fulfillment." Someone that is "self- actualized" by Maslow's definition has a greater sense of morality, creativity, spontaneity, problem solving, a lack of prejudice and the acceptance of facts."

Well, in today's culture we would almost immediately question where the "facts" are coming from and whether they are a believable or credible source. However, I do know people that seem to be "evolved" and are of great character and intelligence and they do in fact accept things that seem to be factual and tend to be less "argumentative," but rather thoughtful and genuine. That is not to be mistaken with many of our public servants that somehow think they are "above" us "normal people" and they can debate on laws that impact us all and are "reasonable" in their discussions and debate. I would ask them to take another look at the "morality" part, because, as we are finding out, more and more of these men and women that go into public service come out very wealthy with great contracts and contacts with multibillion dollar conglomerates and seemingly are "self-actualized" in some ways, but really, deep down are insecure, petty thieves that have created an image or mask to cover their own insecurities.

Interestingly, I equate Maslow's "self-actualization" to Aristotle's description of "happiness" and a "Good Life" in his writings on "Ethics." While terribly dry, as one of the greatest thinkers and philosophers, he makes points that are incredibly accurate even today. In fact, I think his descriptions of public service and character, the "just man" and "the moral man" in "*Nicomachean Ethics*" are sobering and something we should all be required to read, especially those that run for public office.

There are several reasons why I use Bernie Madoff, Tiger Woods, celebrities and public officials as examples when speaking about "esteem" and "self-actualization." As human beings I think we have a view of the world around us and a view of ourselves, separately.

We look outside ourselves and "judge" or "measure" others and who they are, like most other animals as I have referred to previously. Our natural instinct to study someone, I believe is part of our instincts as a human animal. We use our senses and our intuition to determine if someone is a threat or a potential mate. We use our senses that we have developed over our lifetime to determine who we allow into our lives and who to trust. Unfortunately, many times, that "intuition" or sense to avoid people that are harmful to us and our lives is miscast and we allow people into our lives and hearts that will either unintentionally or intentionally do us harm.

On the journey to "self-actualization" there are so many contributing factors and so many things that impact our lives and the aspects that make up our lives that have lead me to the creation of the "*21ˢᵗ Century Multidimensional Hierarchy of Needs.*" As you have read so far, the journey toward "self-actualization" is complex and is influenced by our own genetics and our experiences from the moment we are conceived to the very moment you are reading this sentence. The human experience is a Multidimensional experience and can be measured on a number of different levels.

You could be "Mother Theresa" and be measured for your ability to give and inspire others, but should there be a measurement for financial gain and not living to that potential? If someone intentionally chooses to not participate in some aspect of life, whether it be health and wellness or financial gain does that no longer become a measurement of their "personal fulfillment" in this life? The example of Mother Theresa is a unique one, because she exemplifies so many good things, but how could she be successful at serving others for so long without it serving some personal need of her own as a human being? Therefore, her view of her world and her role in it was a measurement of how she could help people and how many.

"You will get all you want in life if you help enough other people get what they want." Zig Ziglar

Those that are "celebrated" in this life seem to be publicly acknowledged for their "greatness" in one aspect of their life or another:

- Mother Theresa ~ Giving, caring, goodness and "Saint"
- Michael Jackson ~ Music and Dance
- Tiger Woods ~ Golf and "Athlete"
- George Clooney ~ Acting, Looks and Philanthropy
- Sandra Bullock ~ Acting, "Girl next door" and victim
- Warren Buffet ~ Wealth and Philanthropy
- Bill Gates ~ Microsoft / Technology, Wealth and Philanthropy
- Lebron James ~ Basketball and athlete
- Anthony Robbins ~ Motivation
- Heidi Klum ~ Beauty and "The Body"
- Bono ~ Music and Public Policy
- President Bill Clinton ~ Leadership and philanderer

This is just a small list of people that are well known in the public and celebrated figures for a variety of reasons, but they have also had their failings. As much as we look around our world and gather information, whether it be to measure our own "success" or personal fulfillment, it is impossible to look at the "success" of others and determine if they have become "self-actualized" or "personally fulfilled." It is a truly personal journey, but subject to judgment.

We are all born with tremendous gifts. We are all born with "handicaps," whether seen or unseen.

Our personal journey to "self-actualization" and "personal fulfillment" is based on our intentions and focus. When we state that self-actualization is the ability to achieve personal fulfillment and become the very best you that you can be, what does that mean? Is it the ability to live a happy, well balanced and personally fulfilling life? Does it mean living up to your "potential?" What is your potential?

"Neo, there is a difference in walking the path and creating the path." Line from the movie "Matrix"

As I referred to earlier, Dr. Deepak Chopra refers to "pure potentiality." What is that? There are human beings that can do amazing physical things...are we all capable of doing those things under the right circumstances or with the right focus and intensity?

I am dedicating some time to this thought, because this is the genesis, the beginning, the foundation. The "Alpha and the Omega." So, "self-actualization" is seen as the pinnacle or top of the personal development pyramid, but in many ways it is also the "foundation" of all that we do. I have heard this phrase used in a variety of ways, "if you don't know where you are going, any road will get you there." In essence, if you do not have a goal or a direction or an ambition, anything you do will be in the direction of your goal, nowhere. Essentially, "same shit different day." Much like a dog or a cow just meandering through their days allowing their bodily functions and needs be the driving force of their existence. Sustenance. Just living. Does that meet or exceed any standards or equate to a "fulfilled" life?

If someone literally chooses to do nothing and become a 500 pound "couch potato," and is content to live out their existence that way, can that be considered "self-actualization" and a personally fulfilled life?

I believe the answer to that is "no."

We as human beings are given gifts and talents. We all have something that makes us unique to others. I believe that part of our "human experience" is to find what that is and develop it responsibly to the very best of our ability. So, when people refer to "body, mind and spirit," I believe we have a "human responsibility" to take care of our minds, bodies and spirits or souls."

"We are not human beings having a spiritual experience. We are spiritual beings having a human experience."
~ Teilhard de Chardin~

So, as we think and focus on our "human experience" and what it is that we want to be or become and focus on our journey toward "self-actualization"…what is it that we want and how do we go about doing it? I think this is one of the oldest questions asked by mankind and one that eludes so many.

The concept or phrase, "be the best you can be," seems pretty simple and direct. I have always loved the phrase, "theory is great, yet in application." So, in theory, "being the best you can be" is a goal or a way of living. However, every minute of every day focusing on how to be your very best is entirely different in application. Every moment of every day, thinking of how you can be at your best? Wow! Now that's a tough goal, but not specific enough.

If you set a goal that is too abstract and not specific and measureable, you are likely to not achieve it, because there is no specific way of measuring it. So, your "goal setting" should be **SMART**.

S pecific ….set a specific goal
M easureable…your goal should be measureable
A ttainable… the goal should "stretch" you, but not be impossible
R elevant…your goal should be important to you and in the direction of where you are going.
T ime based… your goal should have a definite time frame, like today, this week or month.

The idea of "SMART" goal setting is not a new one, but one that has been unattainable for many.

National Motivation & Inspiration Day®

January 2nd

Goal-setting is one of the reasons I created National Motivation & Inspiration Day©, which I had passed through The United States Congress after the events of September 11, 2001. After 9/11 a lot of things changed, however, the thing that I noticed the most was cooperation. People, Americans, helping each other out. Everyone chipping in to help each other…pushing aside judgments and alienating each other. We all wanted to help each other out, regardless of who you were.

Why would it take a catastrophe or some outside force to make us all respect each other's differences and not care about who you are, but rather, how can I help you. So, this is what National Motivation & Inspiration Day© or "Motivation Day™" is all about.

Only 3% of the population sets written goals for themselves and less than 1% review their goals on a regular basis.

Establishing goals and objectives for life. Every January 2nd, I ask Americans to establish measurable, attainable goals for themselves, SMART Goals. And then strive to achieve them, especially young adults. If we can learn to successfully create SMART, attainable goals and on an annual basis keep achieving them…what aren't we capable of accomplishing? If every year, each one of us has a goal of being healthier and living more contently and "successfully" and we all strive to get to that place and help each other along the way. Like we did for 9/11, what can't we accomplish?

Yes, a little "euphoric" or "Pollyanna" and maybe even naïve, however, if we do not strive for excellence… if we do not try to achieve more, then what is left? Do we all just coast through life only looking out for ourselves on a daily basis with no destination or journey or road map plotted out in front of us? Do we all live by the mantra, "same shit, different day?" That would certainly not be confused with living an "inspired life."

If you are seriously considering joining the 3% of most successful people that write out their personal goals and hold themselves accountable for achieving them, then go to the National Motivation & Inspiration Day web site and download your own personal Success Calendar!

http://www.motivationandinspirationday.org/

Almost, every trip or journey you go on, you plot a route or think of how you are going to get there. Why wouldn't we do that for this most important of journeys, this thing called YOUR life? The next couple of chapters are dedicated specifically to that objective.

Helping U chart a course of success for your life.

4

Breaking Down and Personalizing the 21st Century Multidimensional Hierarchy of Needs

The Set Up

I will reiterate here that I am not a Psychologist or therapist and I am not going to use any "psychobabble." As we discussed earlier in the book, there has been a long argument of "Nature vs. Nurture," …what are you born with and what happens based on your environment. There have been numerous studies on this and it is not an area of expertise or focus, but certainly influences our discussion.

In almost every discussion of psychology there is the influence of your parents. In particular, our poor mothers. So many mothers are blamed for so many poor decisions made by young adults, like somehow the mom's actually made the decision for them. It's pretty amazing and seems to be gaining strength by what I see in today's culture. The influence of parents and "helicopter parents" on this generation will have an interesting impact on our society over the next 20 years. It may very well set us back a generation.

I cannot think of a more critical or important relationship in our lives than the connection we have with our mothers. However, that said, once again, there are a number of people that overcome terrible relationships with their mothers and there are others that take great relationships with their mothers and have horrible and unproductive lives. So, once again this leads me to U.

We are all a product of our genetics and our environment. There is no argument there. However, there are many that use their background and relationships with their parents or mothers as an excuse for their lack of performance. In Gestalt Therapy or in NLP (Neuro-Linguistic Programming), which are both forms of psychotherapy, therapists work with an individual to increase your level of personal accountability and change your perspective to change your own personal behaviors and habit patterns in order to create different outcomes or results.

There has been a popular trend in corporate organizational change and in the professional speaking industry to refer to the definition of "insanity." The definition of insanity is:

> *"doing the <u>same</u> thing over and over again and expecting a <u>different</u> result."*

The obvious disconnect is that it is unrealistic or "insane" to do the same things over and over and expect a different result. Doing things "differently" provides "different results." This also gives birth to the phrase and ideology of "thinking outside the box."

What is being said is that change cannot occur unless you do something different. Whether it be in a corporation or an individual, if you want different results or outcomes, you must change behaviors and activities. This is what creates different results, which change the course of companies and of course changes people's lives.

A very simple example is, if you want to lose weight…you must? Eat less and exercise more, is the popular answer. However, we have found that is not necessarily the correct answer for everyone, because after a couple of weeks or months, people regain all the weight they lost. So, the correct answer is more specific: Eat less "calories" and higher quality, more nutritious food and increase exercise in order to burn more calories than you consume on a daily basis and make this a change in your way of life for good, not just a short period of time.

You can see the distinct difference in these answers. They are similar, but the second answer is far more specific and accurate. As they say, "the devil is in the details," and individuals that are looking to lose weight must have a very specific diet and regimen to follow in order to get the desired results. Weight, "self-esteem" and "self-image" is only one aspect of your overall life though.

My parents were immigrants from Ireland. They believed in "The American Dream" and "upward mobility." They believed if you were well-educated and worked hard you could "make it" in America. They also believed that athletics were important and encouraged us to play sports. In our family's case, that was soccer.

So, if you break those down, "education," "physical well-being," and achievement were valued and critically important in our household. Lord forbid if you weren't a good athlete or driven!

I have also informed you that our dysfunction, as with far too many Irish, immigrant families was alcohol and poverty. There was far too much alcohol drunk that lead to far too many fights and far too little money for ten people to live on.

So, in the case of my personal development and with most children, you have to look at several aspects or areas of your life: Relationships; Physical Being; Sexuality; Mental& Emotional Wellness; Education; Finances and Faith/Religion... a 7-sided pyramid!

Relationships Physical Being Sexuality Mental& Emotional Education Finances Faith/Religion

Certainly the experiences of your young life influence the outcome of who you are and how you see yourself and the world around you. As we have stated earlier, you are given some genetic gifts (nature), which are either enhanced or tarnished, based on the environment (nurture) that you are brought up in. However, there are far too many children of wealthy and privileged people that become drug addicts or alcoholics and far too many people that come from absolutely nothing to become a success that any one rule can be true. Therefore, once again, it is a mixture of the two.

Which brings us back to:

"To thyne own self be true."
William Shakespeare's Hamlet

For many, it is a difficult challenge to get through life. The imbalance of emotional and / or psychological damage, as well as chemical imbalances and of course, legitimate "mental illness" can make life a deeply troubling and emotionally draining experience.

There is a great saying that has been changed several times, so I am not sure which one was first, but it states:

"Life is a journey, not a destination." OR
"Success is a way of life, not a destination."

The process and journey from childhood to young adulthood is pretty seamless. The peer pressure is not too great and the choices are largely made for you by your parents or adults.

The transition, however, from young adulthood to adulthood can be a tricky, slippery, dangerous and treacherous path with many choices. Some of these choices are easy and some of them are very difficult. Notice I use the word "choices," because that is all it is…making the "right" choices. We know that this is easier said than done, however, if you consistently make the "right" choices and follow some fundamental rules and use common sense of what is "right" and "wrong" you should be able to make the transition well.

Most young adults have the belief that things are "different" now than when their parents were kids. It's truly amazing to me that no matter where I go, people truly want to believe that they somehow have some special set of circumstances that do not exist elsewhere. Whether it be a corporate environment or an individual. People take a special sense of pride that their situation is different and that there is no way that there is a simple answer that will address not only their personal situation, but 90% of other situations as well. That would be so, "un-special" or make someone feel like they are not "unique?" How could that be, that one answer could answer the challenges of so many people or companies in so many different places? The answer actually is very simple, because we are all human. The consistent thread is that whether you live or work in Florida, New York, Los Angeles or Seattle, that you are an individual living out your life interacting with a group of other people living out their own lives.

Therefore, there are statistics that can consistently show almost anything. Regardless of your position, as long as there are measureable numbers associated with your discussion, there are statistics to help reinforce your argument. In this case, my "argument" would be with young adults, (14 to 21) that think they or their situation is significantly different than anyone else or any given time and place.

Here is an example:

You could be' dropped into a "normal" High School environment anywhere in America at almost any point in time and break down the High School population into very specific and definable categories.

The most obvious, how many boys vs. girls. How many kids? What is the socio-economic make-up of the school and community? Knowing these pieces of information, you could probably come within a few percentage points of knowing the breakdown of; "dorks" or the really smart kids. "jocks" or the athletes in the school; "druggies" or kids that are known to be involved with drugs and "nobodies" or the rest of the kids that don't really fit in any of these categories. And of course, you would know, based on who you are, where you fit in that population.

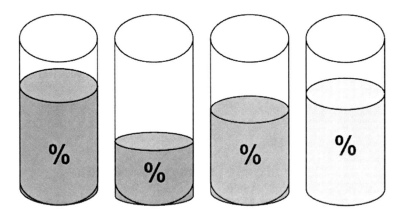

Statistically, things do not change as significantly as you may think. Depending upon the socio-economic indicators and culture of the community, you could make and "educated guess" of what type of kid someone is, what group he or she fits into and what behaviors they are most likely involved in. While this is not "scientific," it is more intuitive, which requires you to trust yourself and trust your ability to judge people accurately. Granted, that jumping to conclusions or making sweeping generalizations about someone or a group of people or kids is not fair, but it happens all the time. These assumptions help guide us in a lot of decisions that we make in our lives, correctly or incorrectly.

Let me reinforce that you are special. Every individual is special in their own way, but that does not mean that you cannot be grouped into a specific "category" or group. While unfair, people love to categorize or generalize about people. Put them in a "box" or category, because then it's easier to fit them into our own sense of seeing the world. For some, the world is a very "black and white" kind of place. For others, the nuances of life and truly understanding the differences between people takes time and energy, but I would have to say that is where you find deeper and more meaningful relationships. We as people however, do not necessarily have the time, nor do we take the time to find out all there is to know about someone and jump to conclusions in order to save time.

The one thing that is significantly different about the current population of young adults (14 to 24), which I believe is a cultural revolution is the use of electronic devices that take over communication.

"93% of all communication is non-verbal."

As human beings, we communicate in a variety of ways. A significant portion of our communication as human beings, 93%, is non-verbal. Our tone, inflection, hand gestures and body language contribute to the words we are using in order for someone to get a better understanding of what we actually mean.

In our current environment, texting and emailing have been explosive in their use and I fear will lead to a communication gap in our society. There are hundreds of billions of text messages and emails sent every day, which may lead to a drastic change in how we communicate. This is only one contributing factor into the overall development in the human experience.

"The quality of your life, is the quality of your communication."
~ Anthony Robbins ~

There are several categories of study that I have introduced in the past several pages that all have experts and people that have spent a lifetime studying and quantifying and I have only introduced concepts in order to not get bogged down in minutia, but these categories are critical to this discussion and to the human experience. I encourage you as an enlightened individual that is looking for answers and open to self-reflection to pick up books on: biology; behavior; business; genetics; philosophy; psychology; faith or religion; and demographics or statistics. There is so much to know and learn. Take the time and energy to expand your mind and your universe so that you can better understand the information I am sharing with you, but also understand yourself and your role in this world.

"Knowledge is Power!"

5

Creating Your Pathway to Personal Success

Earlier in the book, I referred to several aspects of your life:

- Physical Being
- Mental and Emotional state
- School or Work or both
- Finances
- Relationships (parents, siblings, friends, others, etc.)
- Sexuality
- Faith or Religion

Over the next several pages, I would like to provide you with your own personal pathway to success. If we can understand the journey toward self-actualization and we can establish reasonable goals toward the direction of self-actualization and personal fulfillment then hopefully in some small way we can all work toward a better life and a better world.

Creating Your Pathway to Personal Success ~ Physical Being

We are born into this world with one similarity. We are human.

We are all made up of different genetic codes, which provide us with a variety of different talents and aptitudes. Throughout this book, I have referred to the battle of Nature vs. Nurture. If both of

your parents are over 6 feet and came from tall families, it is unlikely that you will be under 6 feet tall. That does not mean, however, that you are automatically a basketball player.

When it comes to your physical body, what do you need in order to get from a level of "physiological" and fundamental function to a level of "self-actualization" and being the very best that you can be in your physical state?

First, we need a starting point. If you are reading this book or old enough to have interest in it, then I will assume that you are least a teenager or older. So, another thing that we can probably agree upon is that while we know we are all human, we also know that our bodies have bone, muscle, cartilage, ligaments and tendons, that all work together to help us move. Each individual has varying strengths of muscles and ligament and tendons and bones to help them perform.

Some move more gracefully than others, but regardless, we can agree that we all move based on the fundamental use of these body parts. Certainly one of the most significant is our muscles and a constant focus for those that are athletes. Those of you that are very active and engaged in regular physical activity probably know most of the fundamentals of how to stay "in shape" or get "in shape." Your challenge becomes how to get the very best of yourself and "become the very best U that U can be." How do you "maximize" your own potential? How do you learn to push your body to the point that it is as strong and as durable as you can make it? And how do you maintain that level of fitness?

Let's face it. Working out is tough. If you're an 18 year old football player that plays a "skill position," which requires, strength, fitness, endurance, agility, speed and muscles so that you don't get hurt, your body type is probably significantly different than that of the All-American cross country runner. The muscles and mechanisms required are significantly different, but they can still both reach a level of physical "self-actualization" or fulfillment just the same. Neither is "better" than the other, just different if they have both learned to maximize the potential of their bodies.

Let's take a closer look at these athletes.

The 18 year old starting quarterback stands 6' 4" inches and is 205 lbs. He has a perfect physique, yes, 6-pack abs and runs the 40 yard dash in 4.5 seconds.

Meanwhile the 18 year old All American Cross Country runner is 5' 9" and 145 lbs. He is slender and fit, yes, 6-pack abs and he runs the 7 mile long course in 34 minutes, which is under 5 minute miles.

Both athletes are superior at what they do and have driven themselves to be the best they can be.

There is another young man on the Cross Country team however, that is a little different. Let's call him Bob. Both of his parents are obese. They have told him that it is not their fault and that it is genetic. They consume massive amounts of food and eat out frequently at fast food restaurants. Bob has chosen to fight this. He made a conscious decision when he was a Freshman in High School (14 years old) that he was not going to just give in and accept that he was destined to be obese like his parents.

When he started running freshman year, the coaches and school doctors were concerned and asked that he go to a Doctor to get approval to run. He started out on the short course and was always last. Bob was 5' 3' and 200 lbs. He pushed himself through the vomiting and feeling sick and the pain he felt in his legs, the embarrassment and teasing and continued to run. He committed to show up every day, even in the cold rain of November. He participated in every team drill and every exercise. He knew he was not as good as most of the kids, but he didn't give up. After the end of the first season, Bob was 5'4" and 190 lbs. He didn't get much of a result from all of his hard work, but he refused to quit and thankfully, he made a few friends along the way on the team that also encouraged him to keep up.

Bob ran on his own all year and all summer preparing for sophomore year. He grew another few inches, but also gained weight. Bob was frustrated by the process, but continued to not give up on himself. He pushed himself to change his body and his future. He refused to be obese like his parents. He didn't eat dinner with them. He spoke with a school dietitian and learned about what he should eat in order to provide his body with enough nourishment, but not all those fat calories. He learned how often to eat and what to eat. By senior year in High School and on his 18th birthday, Bob was 5' 11 and 200 lbs. He did not have the physique of the football player or the All American Cross Country runner, but what Bob had done was reach a level of "self-actualization" and became the very best he could be in his physical being.

This anecdotal story provides a variety of lessons. There are consistencies in achieving excellence in anything that we aspire to do. Remember that Maslow's original hierarchy did not have a Multidimensional component and did not allow for progression or regression within the original hierarchy. So, your physical body and well-being was only one element of your overall wellness and if there was any area where you were not moving toward "self-actualization," you were essentially "stuck" on that level.

The addition of Dr. Clayton Aldefer's ERG Theory to Maslow's original Hierarchy added the concept of "regression theory." That someone that was unable to reach the next level in the hierarchy would fall back into a previous stage and potentially increase or double their effort in order to reach the next level within the hierarchy.

With the addition of the ERG theory, we continue with our little story.

The football player went on to play in college and was seriously injured while playing. After tearing his ACL, MCL, LCL and PCL (all the ligaments that hold the knee together) he stopped playing football. He was the college version of a "has been" and went to a lot of parties, gained a lot of weight and developed a drinking problem.

After college, he blew up to 300 lbs. and spoke a lot about his college career and bounced around as a football coach.

His physical well-being would now be at the lowest level of physiological development, because he is overweight, has heart disease, is an alcoholic and is in serious jeopardy of dying.

The All American Cross Country star went on to college and stopped running competitively his junior year. He was a very good and serious student and with his future of becoming a doctor he had little time for anything else, so he chose to quit running.

He is now a doctor and takes care of himself, but not enough due to time constraints. While he is nowhere near the shape of the football player, he is certainly not "self-actualized" in his physical being as he once was and has thereby dropped back into a moderate level of "belonging" and esteem.

The beauty of life and our journey in it is that as long as we are committed to doing our best and applying effort toward that goal, we can strive and attain self-actualization and become the very best you that you can be. However, that is not the same as saying, "I did the best I could." Most people that say that, use it as an excuse for giving a half-hearted effort.

Bob became a huge success. He learned through his challenges in his younger life about hard work and perseverance. He learned to believe in himself and when he made a commitment to himself, he never gave up.

Bob went to a good school, a state school and got great grades. He didn't join the Cross Country team, but ran every day before school and went to the gym in the evenings. In addition to his Business Degree and MBA, he also obtained a minor in nutrition.

Bob is now an executive at a very large organization and makes nutrition and well balanced food a staple of his company. Every floor has a food station with water, fruits and vegetables that people can take freely as they need to maintain their energy.

He still runs and has completed several marathons. Bob became the success story! His willingness to do the hard work early in his life and set attainable goals and never give up on himself lead him to a life of success. Not only does he maintain his 5' 11" frame at approximately 175 lbs., he has mastered his own physiology and has truly reached a level of "self-actualization" and became "the very best U that he could be."

For more information on becoming the very best physical specimen that you can be, I strongly recommend going to: www.EatWiseandExercise.com

Creating Your Pathway to Personal Success ~ School and Work

"Success" at school and at work requires very similar skills and direction. I will stay clear of discussing "relationships" here, because that is a separate topic. When looking at School and Work success it brings to mind the phrase I share with audiences all across North America, "do what you love and the money will follow."

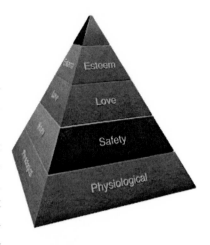

At school, you most likely excel at the things you like and that you may be naturally gifted at. It is not uncommon for people to like things that they are good at and be good at things that they like. After school, if you can find a career that you like and you are good at it will eventually lead you to make money. In this ultra-competitive world you should love what you do, because it will make it easier to get up early and stay up late, as I tell my audiences. Can you imagine being the person that hates what they do? How difficult is it to get up in the morning to go to school or work? How difficult is it to stay at school or work all day and perform to the best of your ability when in fact you can't stand being there? This is your first competitive advantage.

However, it is also important to "stretch" yourself and apply yourself. If you are good at something, you shouldn't take it for granted and not push yourself to be the very best that you can be at it. To be good at something and not apply yourself and "coast" is a sin. Not applying your gifts and talents, whether it be at school or at work is truly short changing yourself, but also short changing the world around you. When people that are good at a specific skill or talent really apply themselves and strive to be the very best they can be it establishes a new standard for everyone else. It may push you to create new things at levels that have never been done before or maybe your contribution will push some uniquely talented person to new heights that will benefit society in some way.

There are those that believe that we are all born with a unique talent and I agree with them. I think every individual on the planet has a "God-given" talent. Because I believe in God, it's easy for me to believe this, but for someone that does not believe in God it may not be. Don't despair. Why are you here? What are you good at? Is there something that you and people within your immediate family seem to have an aptitude for and excel at it? Then, maybe that's a good place to start. That first step of finding comfort and security in your decision is the equivalent of the first step in the "hierarchy of needs." Once you get under way and are doing something you enjoy at school or at work, you can then focus on "satisfying" each need at each of the levels, securely moving toward, "fulfillment," becoming the very best that you can be and "self-actualization" at school or work.

I have had the fortune of meeting young adults all across America that "know what they want to be when they grow up" and I have colleagues that knew what they wanted to be and became exactly that. How cool is that? To know from the time you are a teenager that you want to be a doctor, dentist, lawyer, professional athlete, teacher, singer, entertainer or architect and then become one. To have a central focus and be driven to succeed at an early age…what a wonderful gift.

I have also though, had the misfortune of meeting young adults and adults that do not know what they want to be when they grow up and continue to not know. For those of you reading this that fall into that category, please, do not disconnect, do not get discouraged. As long as you focus your energies toward either work or school and put in the time to learn at some point in time something will "click" and make sense. There are also "tests" that you can take to measure your level of interest and aptitudes toward certain careers and professions. Guidance and Career Counselors at High Schools and Colleges have these tests. Go take one, it can't hurt. It will give you a sense of direction and potential careers that will ignite your interest and passion about your future and what it can hold for you.

Remember though, you must stay focused and committed to what you are trying to achieve. If you approach all of this "half-heartedly" then that is the result you will get.

I was in Florida once conducting a training session and there was a young man, maybe in his mid-20's that shared with us that his Dad told him that "half of life was showing up." That's right; "success" could be his by "showing up!"

"To be or not to be, that is the question."
Romeo & Juliet

The problem with "showing up" is that is says nothing about the "state of mind" that you should show up with. I stated earlier in the book, yes, it's great to determine "to be," but what then? How to be? Are you a person that just "shows up" for life? Or are you someone that is going to live your life to the fullest? Those are two very different lives, I would think.

Your education and career are not for others to judge you, but a way for you to not only pay your way through life, but fund yours and your family's life to the degree that you want to live. I stated earlier, it would be unfair for you to beat yourself up in your mid 20's if you chose not to continue education after High School and you realized that your choices were limited. This would be the same realization of wanting to travel the world and yet your career of choice barely lets you travel to the next state.

If you are a young adult reading this, there is significant information at your fingertips that show you a college education and Master's Degree are an expectation today in most professional "white collar" careers. The fact that Colleges and Universities are profiting at the expense of kids leaving college with a "mortgage" and no jobs is another story. If you have "no interest" in college or really do not enjoy being in a college environment, there are many alternatives and career choices. However, it requires you to be proactive. To say that you "do not like school" and have poor grades to show for it, does not give you the right to waste your time playing video games or "hanging out." That's just misusing your time and being lazy. If you truly want to live a "good life" and have a career and money to support you and your family eventually, then dedicate your time to finding a vocation or career where you do not have to go to college and can still make a decent living. Do internships or coop programs. Volunteer. Spend time exposing yourself to a variety of vocations until you find the one thing that you can't imagine not doing. The thing that "inspires you," ignites a fire inside of you and you can't wait to do it. Once you have found that, then you will find a way to make money and a lifelong career at it or some variation of that activity to make your professional career fulfilling.

Creating Your Pathway to Personal Success ~ Finance

Recently, the global economy has taken a downturn. Here in the U.S., unemployment is at record highs of 10%. People are not only struggling to make ends meet, but their invest-ments have also suffered and property values have plummeted. Sort of a financial "perfect storm."

There are many people that saved for years and owned properties and seem- ingly had done everything "right" and are still in financial ruin. Their cash or liquid investments took a deep loss or were "swindled" as was the case with those that invested with Bernie Madoff. The "mortgage crisis" created a "financial black hole" that impacted Financial Institutions all over the world.

This represents a time in our history that is "similar to" the "Great Depression." That period of history provided a psychological mindset for many people of that generation. Older people describe themselves as "babies of the great depression" when describing the reason why they don't spend money or why they save money. The lack of money and the poverty and helplessness that was created in America marked a generation.

So too will our current financial situation. There are young men and women that are being born into the current economic struggle that will be marked by the economic challenges. Will they be "better" with their money? Will they not invest it? Will they only use cash? We do not know the impact of our current economic crisis upon this generation, nor will we know for 50 years until they are older.

The intention of this chapter however, is to provide some fundamental guidance of how to move beyond each of the "levels" and satisfy the "need" at each level toward "personal fulfillment or "self-actualization." With people like Bill Gates, Warren Buffet and Oprah in the world it is hard to say a $ dollar amount that means "you have made it!" or calculating what you are "capable" of making based on your experience, education and family background. Lord knows, Bill Gates did fine as a college dropout.

So, when addressing the question of "personal finances," there isn't a calculation that will provide you with a "number" that you need to make in order to become "self-actualized," however, as human beings we certainly do make judgments when someone "over achieves" or makes more money than we thought they were capable of making.

Creating Your Pathway to Personal Success ~Relationships

From the day we are born, our life is a constant interaction with other people.

As an active member of society it is impossible to get through life without interacting with other human beings. There are a number of descriptions that people use for themselves, such as, shy, quiet, reserved, outgoing, friendly, fun and the list goes on. There are also a number of "generalizations" that people make about their own "personality" and others.

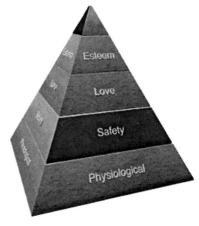

Probably the most well-known generalization about people is the use of the phrase, an "A-type personality." What does that mean exactly? What is an "A type" personality? What is a "personality?"

Interestingly, there are a variety of descriptions on Dictionary.com for "personality." *–noun, plural* -ties.

1. the visible aspect of one's character as it impresses others: *He has a pleasing personality.*

2. **a person as an embodiment of a collection of qualities:**
He is a curious personality. *Psychology* **the sum total of
the physical, mental, emotional, and social characteristics of an individual.**

  b. the organized pattern of behavioral characteristics of
  the individual.

3. the quality of being a person; existence as a self-conscious
human being; personal identity.

4. the essential character of a person.

5. something apprehended as reflective of or analogous to
a distinctive human personality, as the atmosphere of a
place or thing: *This house has a warm personality.*

6. a famous, notable, or prominent person; celebrity.

7. application or reference to a particular person or particular
persons, often in disparagement or hostility.

8. a disparaging or offensive statement referring to a
particular person:
The political debate deteriorated into personalities.

It would seem that definition #2 would be the most accurate for
our discussion. A "personality" is an accumulation of "physical, mental, emotional and social characteristics." So, when we
describe a person's "personality" or our own, we are incorpor
ating all of the things that make that person an individual.

For several years I have dedicated some time in understanding "human behavior" and "behavioral styles," which I have
used in a number of my programs with management groups
and for individual success training. There are several different types of "Behavioral Style Measurement" programs, such
as, Myers Briggs, Platinum Rule and DISC.

I happen to prefer the DISC Behavioral Style Measurement
Tool, because of its simplicity. However, there are now many

variations of behavioral measurement programs on the market. Regardless of what is used, as long as it provides an accurate assessment of an individual's "be havioral style" it can be used successfully for individual growth.

The importance of "behavioral style measurement" in relationships is that when you have a better understanding of who you actually are, then you can have a better understanding of why you relate to various people differently.

In the DISC Behavioral Measurement tool there are Four Behavioral Styles to figure out. There are some fundamental differences between the four styles and it contributes to what kind of relationships you have with each "behavior type." Keep in mind that these are described as "behavioral styles" and not "personalities." And most people are a mixture of these "behavioral styles." Only 2% of the population is dominantly just one behavioral style. Therefore, we are all a mixture of "styles" that lead to our "behavior."

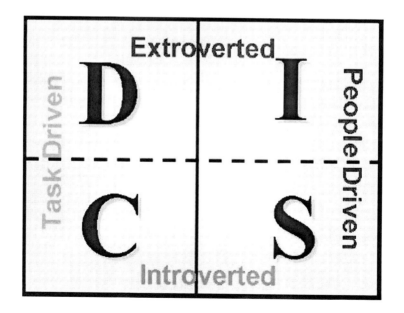

Understanding the Graph

The "**D**" and "**I**" behavioral styles are above the dotted line and are considered "extroverted" or "outgoing" behavioral styles, while the "**C**" and "**S**" are considered "introverted" behavioral styles.

The "**D**" and "**C**" styles to the left are considered "Task Oriented" styles and the "**I**" and "**S**" behavioral styles to the right are considered "People Driven" behavioral styles.

Understanding the four DISC behavioral Styles

"**D**" Behavioral Styles are referred to as being "driven" or "direct." You might consider this the generalized description of an "A type personality." They tend to be "extroverted" and outgoing and "task driven." They are driven to get things done.

"**I**" Behavioral Styles are considered, "people…people." "I's" love to be around people and are also "extroverted" and outgoing and are "people centered." They love to be with other people.

"**S**" Behavioral Styles have a "serving" nature. No, that is not the same as being a "servant." It is just pleasing and natural to them to give and take care of others. They too are "people driven" like "I's," but they tend to be "introverted" and a little more reserved in their nature.

"**C**" Behavioral Styles have an "analytical" nature. They tend to want specifics, details and documentation in order to be comfortable and are also "introverted." Like "D's" they are "task oriented," however, unlike "D's" they are not in a hurry to get things done, they want it done, "right" according to their research.

It is important once again to reinforce that we are all a combination of several of these behavioral types. So, a mixture or "chemistry set" of these different styles.

How does this affect our relationships?

Well, let's take the interaction of a "High D" and a "High C" for example. Remember they are both "task oriented," which you would assume is a good thing right? Well, that is the challenge. A "high D" wants to get things done and get them done quickly so they can move onto the next task at hand, while the "high C" may require more time and details. The "high C" might be considered at times, a "devil's advocate." Meaning they may desire bringing up various factoids or even potential challenges associated with a project and specific details of how to address them. This can frankly be infuriating for a "high D" unless they learn how to manage their drive.

Unfortunately for "High D's" they can be considered overbearing and impatient. While being "driven" to accomplish can be a great thing, if it is not balanced properly, it can alienate others. I had a very good friend and "mentor" once tell me, "a strength overused becomes a weakness."

"a strength overused becomes a weakness."

This scenario between a 'High D" and "High C" helps to highlight how relationships can be strengthened or destroyed based on your "behavioral style." If you understand who you are and what your "strengths" and "weaknesses" are, then you can make adjustments to your own behavior to help your relationships go more smoothly.

There are a couple of perfect examples of this that are both positive and negative.

Salespeople are wonderful at adjusting their "behavioral styles" and "personalities" to fit any situation. Understanding when to "turn up" the charm or when to "turn it down." When to provide more details and specifics and when to gloss over specific information to get the sale. The positive of this is that a great salesperson can "fit in" almost anywhere and get along with a variety of other "personalities" or "behavioral styles." Great salespeople are often referred to as "chameleons" for their ability to blend with their surroundings. This can also be dangerous, because sometimes salespeople will do "anything" to make the sale and as someone that is trying to do business with them, you cannot be sure if they are being disingenuous or not. Politicians are examples of "great salespeople." This leads to the terrible joke;

> **"How do you know a politician is lying? …**
> **their lips are moving."**

DISC and other behavioral style measurement programs have simple "tests" that you can take, which are accurately referred to as "assessments." I like the use of "assessment," because that is what it is calling you to do. A "Self-Assessment." What are your "strengths" and "weaknesses" and how can I adjust them in order to have better relationships.

As I have referred to throughout this book, one of the biggest contributing factors to who you are is a mixture of "nature" and "nurture." While your "nature" may be an "I," depending upon the environment that you were brought up in may cause variations to that "nature."

We learn so many things from our parents, because they are our "first teachers." We learn from their behaviors, their language and how they treat us and other people around them. If you have been raised in a "dysfunctional" or "abusive" environment, (I once again suggest therapy and discussing your life challenges with a qualified therapist,) this may unfortunately, negatively influence the nature of who you are. Your nature may be to be a "High I," but because of your upbringing, you do not allow people in and are not trusting of other people.

If you remember, "High I's" are "people…people." So, you can see what kind of "conflict" this would create for someone.

And…unless you take the time to learn about your own "behavioral style" and what your nature is…and take the time to meet with a qualified therapist to discuss some of the dysfunctions in your life, you may be destined to repeat the same type of "abusive" and "dysfunctional" behavior. I refer to this as "hitting the vacuum." You can only go as far as you know and learn. When you go beyond what you have learned and know to be true, you hit a vacuum, which typically resorts back to what you learned at a young age.

For example, how many of us, "learn" or "know" how to be parents? And yet, most adults have children and "learn" how to be "parents" as they go. What is the closest example for each of us of how to be a parent? Our parents and how we were raised. We can try to adjust, because we think our parents did a terrible job or we can try to actively imitate our parents, because we think they did a great job. When you hit the "vacuum of unknowing" you resort to what you have learned almost instinctually, which can lead to the reenactment of your own childhood. You take on the role of the parent that raised you, because you have not taken the time to actually learn another alternative.

Being a "parent" is certainly instinctual in many ways, but when we learn how to combine those loving instincts with more knowledge about how to be a "good parent" and teach our children the fundamentals of feeling secure, being loved, having a healthy self-esteem and know the difference of "right" and "wrong" we are in some ways actually applying the "21st Century Multi-Dimensional Hierarchy of Needs" for our children.

If we take the time to break down each of the components of the hierarchy and analyze how we are actually "meeting the need" then we are consciously acknowledging the importance of each level and how to fulfill the need before moving to the "next level" of behavioral development.

If you look at the "requirements" to "satisfy" each level of the hierarchy, it is here where you can create your own "personal solution" of how to effectively satisfy each level.

For instance: At the "Physiological Level" of relationships, you would essentially have to declare that the "relationship" exists. That's all really.

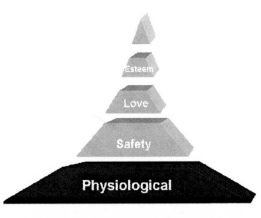

The next level of "Safety" would require you to determine if this is a safe or secure relationship? At the next level of "Love or Belonging" you would determine if this relationship has meaning or has a deeper connection. Not all "relationships" are "Love" relationships, but to meet the "need" at this level there has to be some significant value to the relationship.

At the "Esteem" level of your relationship you can determine if there is "mutual respect." As I referred to Bernie Madoff earlier in the book, here is where you have a challenge. You musthave some trust in yourself and your ability to determine if someone is being honest and being themselves. Most of us have been fooled at some point in time by a "personal" or "professional" relationship where we are lied to and what we thought was a "mutually respectful" relationship was a lie. It is important that whether this is an intimate personal relationship or a long term professional relationship, you must take the time to know this other person. If the "relationship" has "satisfied" the "need" and analysis at each level and you feel secure in trusting the relationship, then you are advancing toward a more fulfilling and evolved relationship.

By the time you reach a "self-actualized" and fulfilling relationship with another person, personally or professionally it will seem effortless. There will be automatic trust, mutual respect and a sense of confidence and security that this associate; friend or lover would not betray you and is someone that you can trust. If you are lucky, we have but a handful of these in a lifetime. Keep in mind, there are some significant differences and steps between personal and professional relationships. However, it is also not uncommon for people that work together to "cross the line" of intimacy, because of these simple hierarchical steps.

Creating Your Pathway to Personal Success ~ Sexuality

Sex... ahhhh! So many people find this topic to be so sensitive and become terribly embarrassed even at the mention of it. Sex.

Well, as I had shared with you earlier, I was once given the "impromptu speech" of "sex" as a senior in High School. While my teacher thought he would throw me off or have fun with the topic at my expense, I was able to change the discussion.

There are two discussions of sex. Gender, Male or Female and of course the other, which is the act or acts that so many people get embarrassed about.

The "gender" discussion of "male" or "female" should be self-explanatory, except for the current day preoccupation with who is "gay" or "not gay" and whether it is something that happens genetically or chemically or is a choice at all.

So, because this is not a "given." As a parent, an adult or even as a young adult, maybe you should take the process through the hierarchy and determine the level of "comfort" with your "sex." Once again, for me, the most important thing that you can take away from this book is a better and greater sense of self in this world. If you are not "comfortable" being "YOU," then who else is going to be comfortable around you?

In Maslow's original hierarchy, he states that "sex" is one of our fundamental "physiological" needs. As an adult human animal, "sex" is a need. However, what about the identity of your "sex." Do you see yourself as a "man" or "woman." I hate the popular phrase about "being in touch with your feminine side" if you are a man. How about just being a caring, sensitive, empathetic and evolved man? It doesn't have to involve any femininity, which is where you end up losing a bunch of men, just because of the label.

Outside of the physical differences between the genders we should all be trying to move toward a place of evolution, which is not "male" or "female," but rather a combination of the two. The discussion of which is "better," being a man or woman just shows how far we have to evolve. That is a discussion to have when you're 10 years old.

Our current societal dilemma is how do we help our children feel comfortable with themselves? Boy or Girl…Male of Female? Gay or Straight.

I am reminded of the story of United States Congressman and Speaker of the House of Representatives, Newt Gingrich. He was openly critical of gays and gay marriage and was complaining about certain group of protestors of California's Proposition 8. Gingrich certainly has his opinions and is an intelligent man and yet, when his sister came out and said she was gay, well, his opinion became far less vocal.

The discussion of whether someone is "gay" or 'straight" is irrelevant. When it touches our lives we all have a change of heart or how we feel about it. The discussion should be about healthy people that are comfortable being themselves and are contributing to society in a positive way.

Our responsibility as adults is to help and mentor children on how to become more confident, secure and comfortable with themselves.

Now, not to pretend that I have an answer, but just like Newt Gingrich being vocal about his position, I think Hollywood has done an equally aggressive and offensive job of "promoting gay lifestyle." All I mean by this is, watch TV for a week. You would think that it is almost abnormal to not have a "gay couple" in your life or in your family. They are trying to influence a generation by having it on so many shows that it just seems common place. That's overkill too.

Back to the challenge at hand. How do we get our kids to become healthy, confident, productive adults?

Lets break it down again.

The Physiological fact is that there are boys and girls, which become men and women. Many children and young adults are "self-conscious" for a variety of reasons, many of which have nothing to do with "sex," but with who they are. Exactly how some children are "bullied" they are also teased about being too: tall, skinny, fat, stupid, gay…whatever kids tease each other about, that is what makes some kids uncertain. Also, once again and unfortunately, some kids are uncertain and don't like themselves, because of how their parents raised them. They are insecure and uncertain, which prevents them from satisfying the next step of "safety."

When our children are at the "Safety Stage" they should feel secure. They should feel safe being in their home and around their family or where they live. Your home should be the "cocoon" the shelter that our children need from the outside world, because we all know that the "real world" can be tough out there.

"the world is just waiting to kick your ass.
That is why "home" should be safe."

The next step of "love and belonging" is where we run into some challenges, both for "bullying" and for anyone that does not fit into the generally accepted behaviors for "sex" and "sexuality."

Remember, once again, as "pack animals" we watch each other very carefully and when things are a little different, they become a focal point.

Think of the transition from childhood to adulthood. It happens from as early as 10 or 11 and continues until 20, 21 even 22 years old. Young adults are changing right before our eyes. Young girls typically "blossom" first and begin to have figures. Nobody says anything? Of course not. Mean girls and boys say nasty things that make them feel insecure and lose a sense of esteem. Girls become insecure about the development of their bodies and want to cover them or not be touched. While of course, there are always the other girls that can't wait to share their newly found bodies because of insecurity and are given appropriate names for doing so. Boys go through their development and many get acne or other growth related challenges and are picked on for being too small or too big (typically not, because they use physical intimidation to not be teased).

So, here, this level of "Safety" and "love and belonging" is where we must help our children evolve better. We aren't even close to discussing "sexual preference" at this point, we're just trying to become. This transition from young adult to adult and these levels of "safety" and "love / belonging" and "esteem" are the most difficult in the human experience.

For those reading this that remember going through this period of time with ease should feel blessed. We must also learn how to harness that experience. What percentage of children / young adults transition well to adulthood and how can we duplicate it. Coming out of this transition intact and in "one piece" is something we should be striving for.

If we can get our young adults to transition through the stages of the hierarchy and get to the level of "esteem" and gaining mutual respect with others that are different than they are, we will have accomplished a lot.

There are many instances in life where we refer to the 80 / 20 Rule. And there are many applications where the 20% becomes the focus. In this case, it may be hard to get a true picture or measurements of what percentage of our young adults are "uncertain about their sexual orientation." I am addressing this, because it is a critical component of development, as well as a significant "battle ground" in modern day society.

I think it is safe to say that most young adults are nervous about their sexuality to begin with. Regardless if they are "gay'" or "straight," they are nervous and uncertain. There have been movements for abstinence, which is in line with many of our religious beliefs, but not as practical as we would like. The abstinence movement is driven just as much to avoid teen pregnancy as it is for religious reasons.

This does not address those that are uncertain of their sexuality and it causes friction and challenges and bullying that is detrimental to these young adults.

Regardless of which side you sit on, there is a "moral dilemma" here.

On the "right" they would have you believe that you are a sinner and would rather you conceal your true self so that we don't have to look at it or have it in public.

On the "left" they would have "gay and lesbian" couples on every TV Show or in every movie and in every street so that you can't ignore it and the influence being that this is something acceptable and "everyone's doing it" kind of mentality.

I personally believe that it has led to the current day culture where you have young women constantly being pictured together either kissing or being photographed together in intimate pictures. That crossing the line and being "bi" or being with another woman is somehow cool or chic, because it's in the movies and on TV.

As adults, I would like to think that we can all agree that we have licenses for driving and you have to be 21 to drink, but the most significant damage to a young person's life can come by being to promiscuous, which leads to either disease or pregnancy. Both will change lives forever…and that should be our focus.

So, as we look at this side of the multidimensional pyramid we must focus on what's most important and not be distracted by propaganda or people trying to "promote" their beliefs as "right." In the end result, the human experience requires us to advance toward something and in this case I am suggesting that the "advancement" is toward "self-actualization" and "personal fulfillment." Regardless if you are "gay" or "straight" in your sexuality, it doesn't need to be anyone else's business. Your "sexuality" is just that, YOURS. The deviance of public ludeness and promiscuity are calls for attention from people with unhealthy beliefs. If you have the need to show your sexuality in public or on the Internet for people to see, you are compensating for an unhealthy sense of sexuality and your own false belief system, which is another issue.

For anyone that feels that they are "trapped" or "caught" between two worlds and are truly uncertain of whether you are "gay" or not. I encourage you to speak to your parents and find a counselor that doesn't have a predisposed opinion, like going to a "gay counselor" or going to a "priest." Go to a professional therapist that can talk you through the process so that you can find your own answer.

In the end, the development of your "sexuality" is important and starts at an early age, however, the choice of being "sexually active" can wait until you are in your 20's if need be… there is no expiration date on your sexuality and there is no shame in being true to yourself.

Creating Your Pathway to Personal Success ~ Faith/Religion

I am a Roman Catholic. My parents were Roman Catholic and I assume that their parents were Roman Catholic. I wrote earlier that my parents were Irish immi- grants. My mother grew up in Northern Ireland. My father grew up in Ireland. I understand religious conflict.

Unbelievably, there are people reading this book that will be turned off by the fact that I am Catholic. They have no idea who I am and have never met me in person, but will be offended that I have stated that I am Catholic. The same would be true if I stated that I was Muslim, Protestant or Jewish. Other, less established religions, might get the response, what's that?

My faith and belief system does not have to be yours. I do not have the answers to all things on this earth. However, I believe that a component of the "human experience" is to have faith in something bigger than ourselves. I just happen to believe that is God and that Jesus was his son.

Does that make me a better person or a "holier person?" Of course not. The answer will come to all of us in due course. My belief is that when I die, I will stand before the "pearly gates" of heaven and be judged. God has given me a certain set of skills and abilities. He has thrown a number of challenges at me in my lifetime. The judgment will be, "how did I do?" Did I do the best with what God gave me? Have I honored him by honoring his creations (people, animals and this world) to the best of my ability. Have I become "self-actualized" and "personally fulfilled?"

I believe these are the questions that we all must ask ourselves and the purpose of this book.

Who are U? and why are you here?

My faith tells me that I should treat others as I would like to be treated; I shall not kill; I shall not steal; I shall not commit adultery, I shall not covet my neighbors goods nor his wife. These are very similar values in most religions. How is it that we have so many conflicts in the world based on religious beliefs? In what religion or religious book does it state that you should kill others that do not believe what you do?

I have chosen to follow the religion or faith that my parents taught me. I didn't have to. I have disagreements with the Catholic Church and some of the things they have done, but last time I checked, I am not The Pope. I cannot pick and choose the rules of the religion that I belong to and say they are wrong about everything else. The Church and its development is the business of far more spiritual and faithful followers than I. It is my job to do the very best I can.

However, for those of you that are unhappy in your "religious beliefs" and want to become something else or follow someone else. Once again you can go through the process of taking the steps of the hierarchy.

The physiological choice to have faith or not have faith. To choose religion or be an Atheist. There are also many that make the choice to be "spiritual." They pray, but not in a Church or building. There is no specific "God" that they pray to, but rather maintain a sense of "spiritual harmony." Does this serve its purpose and will it get you where you want to go? Or is this and "easy way out" or a "cop out," because you do not want to make the time commitment of a traditional religious belief?

Once you have made this choice, what is your level of "safety" or security within that environment? Are you comfortable and secure in your belief and faith. Is it empowering and uplifting? Or, do you feel uncertain and insecure. You don't really believe what your faith stands for or teaches.

At this point is where you actually believe or don't believe and can make the decision to continue on this journey.

When you choose to believe and follow you can now advance to the levels of "love / belonging" and "esteem." What are the friendships and relationships associated with this faith? Are these similarly minded people and do you like / enjoy being associated and connected to them? Are your beliefs congruent with your behaviors and the activities of this faith or religion? If this is true, you will then be prepared for the next level of "Esteem" and creating "mutual respect" with others. Your level of mutual respect for those in your faith will grow and will hopefully evolve into a productive religious faith driven environment where you truly believe you are serving "the greater good."

Once you have fully embraced your faith and have learned it and are surrounded by like-minded people, you can make the next step or advancement toward personal fulfillment and "self-actualization." Truly committing yourself to your faith and community, because this is what you believe to be true.

Creating Your Pathway to Personal Success ~ Mental and Emotional State

The focus of this book is on those that have the ability to read the material and understand the fundamental message and have the ability to apply what you have read. I have not dedicated time to "special interests" or "special needs." While the National Institute on Mental Health suggests that approximately

1 in 4 people or 25% of the population could qualify with some form of "mental illness" at any time in their lives, I am intentionally focusing on the other 75%. Call me crazy.

> *"Whatever the mind of man can perceive*
> *and believe he can achieve."*
> *~ Napoleon Hill ~*

There have been many books and many people that have dedicated their lives to help people understand the power of the mind. One of the founders of the modern day "motivational" movement was Napoleon Hill. He interviewed hundreds of the most successful men in the world and learned about their success.

We currently have one of the most successful and prolific "motivational speakers" and "personal coaches" of all time living in America, Anthony Robbins. He has dedicated his life from the age of 19 years old learning how people learn and apply information. How successful people do it correctly and he has learned how to duplicate it.

Many of the lessons being taught by Napoleon Hill, Tony Robbins, Dr. Wayne Dyer, Zig Ziglar, Dr. Stephen Covey, Deepak Chopra and so many more can be found in a book I mentioned earlier that was written in 350 B.C. by Aristotle. Aristotle's, "*NicomacheanEthics*" provides some of the foundations for "personal success" and motivation, as well as the original ideas of the "Law of Attraction," which Aristotle refers to as "an aether amongst men."

Therefore, "motivation," the "psychology of success" and your mental and emotional state all work together in propelling you toward successfully attaining your goals. If you are coming from a place of pure curiosity and truly interested in becoming "self-actualized" in your mental and emotional state there are several things that I can suggest.

The quote from Napoleon Hill wraps up the simplicity of the thought. "whatever the mind of man (woman) can <u>perceive</u> and <u>believe</u>, he (she) can <u>achieve</u>." This would be considered an "affirmation."

In this simple equation is becomes:

Perception + Belief = Success

Unfortunately my friends that is only half the story. There is another great saying about success. "Success is <u>preparation</u> meeting <u>opportunity</u>."

This equation would be:

Preparation + Opportunity = Success

Once again, close, but no cigar. There is more to it than just thinking it or having an affirmation. Success is also more than simply believing you can. In the 80's as the Berlin Wall was coming down, we began to get a glimpse of what then East Germany was doing with their athletes to create success. Besides steroids, they were using mental imagery to increase the performance of their athletes. Coaches would help them learn to envision success. Envision yourself with the perfect performance and the crowds roaring and you wearing the gold medal. The visualization empowered them with a greater level of confidence, which helped them have an air of superiority and success. Tiger Woods has a process that he was taught by his father. Before striking the ball, he was trained to stand behind it and envision where he wanted it to land before he addressed the ball.

"Begin with the end in mind." **Dr. Stephen Covey**

So now we have a series of things that can help lead us to success...it's just a matter of "syntax or order. What do you think of first in order to win or succeed? Well, you have to envision winning. So, whether you have "won" before or not...you know what it looks like or possibly feels like.

And if you can envision completing the task or competition successfully, that means that you have done the activity before. Here's your challenge. Many people use the phrase, "practice makes perfect." When the reality is, you can practice the same thing over and over again and do it poorly every time. Therefore, your "practice" will never create "perfection."

"Perfect practice, makes perfect." Harvey Mackay

So, now, the equation is becoming a little clearer:

Perceiving Success + "Perfect Practice" + Believing you can succeed + Opportunity =?

Are these the elements of success? Is there anything missing? Well, there are still many intangibles that contribute to success or failure at any given time, but like Michael Jordan the great basketball player pointed out in a 1980's Nike commercial, he failed a number of times. However, those failures are what propelled him toward success.

Therefore. It is critical for you to realize that while you may have made all the "right" moves and done all the hard work and have been presented with an opportunity and still lose, that does not make you a "loser." Only when you choose to quit on yourself do you become a "loser." If you lose n event or an opportunity, while it may hurt or be distracting it is critically important that you take the time to determine what you can learn from the situation and how to prevent it from happening in the future so that you might reach your ultimate goal of success.

Conclusion

The Application
of
The 21st Century Multidimensional
Hierarchy of Needs

The 21st Century Multidimensional Hierarchy of Needs model, like Maslow's original Hierarchy of Needs has application in a variety of areas.

Management & Leadership ~ the multidimensional hierarchy of needs enables managers and leaders to truly look at the depth of their team and measure their performance on a variety of levels to determine not only what "motivates" or drives individuals to peak performance, but also provides opportunity to really evaluate the entire person that you lead or manage not just as an employee. It also empowers leaders with a clear path of how to inspire those that they will lead to victory. What is important to them and what do they believe to be true. Depending on how you measure them or they see themselves at various levels can determine what next steps you need to take. Both Hitler and Martin Luther King took advantage of these things in their rise to power. Obviously one bad and one good.

Education ~ education, learning, teaching and mentoring are all examples of sharing knowledge. The ongoing pursuit of obtaining knowledge and learning your entire life is a sign of an enlightened and potentially "self-actualized" human being.

"the more I learn, the more I know what I do not know."

We teach our children the "three R's," reading, writing and arithmetic, but we do not teach them about themselves? Through the 21st Century Multidimensional Hierarchy of needs we can teach children to break down very simple and fundamental aspects about themselves and their lives in order to find answers that would otherwise be buried for years and cause mental and emotional scarring that isn't uncovered until adulthood.

Parenting ~ the joke has been said many times that you need a license to drive or buy a gun, but anyone can have children. The problem with that is we continue to pass along the mistakes that have been made in this generation to future generations. We do not take the time or effort to educate parents on how to be "better" parents. This philosophy, however, can be challenged, because once again, based on the scientific discussion of "Nature vs. Nurture" we do not know how parental influence motivates a child. There are too many "exceptions" of people that have come from "poor upbringings" to become very successful and too many "wealthy upbringings" have produced underachieving adults.

The use of The 21st Century Multidimensional Hierarchy of Needs, empowers parents with simple steps to follow that uncover their own personal "weaknesses" and makes them aware of how they are potentially influencing their children negatively. Regardless of where a child is raised, if we educate them at an early enough age of how they work, then maybe we can influence what kind of "parents" they will be. What kind of influence would this have and what kind of impact would it have within two or three generations?

Sales & Marketing ~ as with Maslow's original "Hierarchy of Needs," the ability to understand how sales and marketing impact consumers are a key to revenue generation. The 21st Century Multidimensional Hierarchy of Needs does much of the same thing, but now provides an easier and clearer model to evaluate marketing and sales on a niche basis and possibly have greater influence on the analysis of consumer behavior.

Conclusion

The "System" for U
The 5 Essential Steps to Personal Success

People use a variety of "analogies" in life or metaphors to represent situations. You have no doubt heard someone refer to "Overcoming obstacles" or "jumping hurdles in life. Life it seems therefore is a series of "hurdles" that we must "clear" in order to "advance" with our lives.

The 21st Century Multidimensional Hierarchy of Needs is no different, however, I want to provide you with a "process" of clearing these symbolic "hurdles."

In Dr. Maslow's original model of the "Hierarchy of Needs," we were really only focused on one dimension of hurdles and working our way through life trying to "meet the needs" of each level of his original triangle, which was a one dimensional model.

The 21st Century Multidimensional Hierarchy of Needs takes into consideration the complexity of our modern day existence and faces the realization that you are not only "overcoming hurdles" in one dimension, but several and it is not on just one plane, but on several. Kind of like running four, five or six lanes of a track at the same time on several different levels.

Relationships   Physical Being   Sexuality   Mental& Emotional Education   Finances   Faith/Religion

Let's refer to the five original levels of need in Maslow's Hierarchy as levels, 1,2,3,4 and 5 being the top level of fulfillment or self-actualization. And let's use the example from earlier in the book that we are going to "measure" our level of satisfaction in a variety of aspects in our life, such as; Relationships, Physical being, Sexuality, Mental & Emotional well-being; Education / Career, Finances and Faith / Religion. In different stages and phases in our life, for example, 20's, 30's, 40's or 70's or married vs. not married (divorced) or switching jobs or careers, we may have varying levels of "success" meeting the "needs" of these different aspects of life.

For instance, seen below. In our early 20's, we may sense that we are at the following levels of meeting our needs in these variously critical aspects of life: Relationships 1; Physical Being 5; Sexuality 1; Mental & Emotional well-being 4; Education 4; Finances 1; and Faith a 5.

| 1 | 5 | 1 | 4 | 4 | 1 | 5 |
| Relationships | Physical Being | Sexuality | Mental& Emotional | Education | Finances | Faith/Religion |

However, later in life, let's say in our 40's, we are not guaranteed to be at higher levels of "satisfying our needs" just because we are older. In fact, life throws many difficult challenges our way, such as marital issues, financial challenges, health issues and crisis. So, while we assume that there would be obvious areas of growth, because we were in our 20's, now in our 40's we see ourselves or measure at these levels of satisfaction:

| 4 | 3 | 3 | 4 | 3 | 3 | 4 |
| Relationships | Physical Being | Sexuality | Mental& Emotional | Education | Finances | Faith/Religion |

With the advancement of time does not necessarily mean the advancement in our development as a human being. In fact, we may now feel that we are worse off than we were in our 20's.

So, how do we fix this? How do we prevent living lives of "quiet desperation" or the "same shit different day" mentality? How do we live a life to it's fullest continually striving to be the very best that we can be every day until we reach our end goal of becoming "self-actualized" or fulfilled in every aspect of life that we feel requires being met in order to find happiness and contentment.

Whether you choose to "measure" your level of "satisfaction" in the seven aspects of life we use in our example or whether you use fewer or more categories there is a process that you can apply to help you move toward personal fulfillment and a sense that you have "***become the very best U that U can be.***"

STEP 1: Basic Human Need

Regardless of what aspect of life you are looking at, physical, emotional, career, faith / spiritual or sexual you must first understand the lowest level of expectation. Take the exercise of breaking down the "basic need."

Maslow's lowest level of "Physiological Need" is that of existence or sustenance. As an adult (assume over 18) are the "fundamental needs" of "existence" being met in the most critical areas or aspects of your life?

Relationships ~ do you have any meaningful relationships and are you managing these relationships at this lowest level?

Physical Being ~ is your body fundamentally healthy and you can move without restriction?

Sexuality ~ is your fundamental, physical need for sex being met.

Mental & Emotional Well Being ~ are you fundamentally of sound mind and make reasonable judgments and conclusions?

Education ~ are you learning what you need to know to survive or are you having difficulty learning and taking in valuable information?

Finances ~ do you have the fundamental amount of money to exist?

Faith / Religion ~ are you practicing any faith / religion or praying at all?

If you feel that you are successfully meeting or exceeding the "need" of each of these levels then you are prepared to take a look at the next level, 2, which is "safety."

STEP 2: Safety and Security

If you feel that you are at the first and most fundamental level of existence in any of these areas, as many people around the world are, you must first, not judge or be ashamed, but rather be kind and understanding. As you break down what makes up the "needs" at this level, you can uncover what must be met in order to rise to the next level.

In the "safety stage" there is a need for feeling secure. As stated earlier in the book, there are too many people that actually live at this level. They live in fear of personal attack, gangs, threats, intimidation, "bullying", terrorists, rapists and being fired or failing. Literally living in fear.

So, in staying consistent with our examples in each category, how would you determine your level of concern for safety and therefore your ability to satisfying the need at this level of "Safety":

Relationships ~ you do not feel constantly concerned about the "stability" of your relationships and preoccupied with whether they are in jeopardy?

Physical Being ~ you feel "secure" in your "own skin" and not constantly preoccupied with how you look or how others see you.

Sexuality ~ you feel comfortable with yourself and your own sexuality.

Mental & Emotional Well Being ~ a consistent feeling of calm, security and not constantly preoccupied with safety concerns or a state of angst.

Education ~ whether it be in school or at work, are you learning and retaining the things you need to know in order to stay employed or stay in school?

Finances ~ do you have enough money to live

Faith / Religion ~ you are at ease with your faith and the practice of it.

STEP 3: Belonging and Love

Once you have successfully "satisfied" the need for "security" or "safety" in each level of your life that we have measured so far, what's next?

The next couple of levels of "love and belonging" and "esteem" in the Hierarchy are far more complex and nuanced. This is where I believe most people are "stuck." Very few people evolve beyond this level because of a preoccupation in our modern day society about what other people think and how that makes us feel. It is not just "peer pressure," but a mental, emotional and a societal need to "fit in" and not be rejected.

Relationships ~ you "belong" to specific groups of people comfortably and are not concerned with "being yourself."

Physical Being ~ you feel good about your body image.

Sexuality ~ you are comfortable with your sexuality and those around you.

Mental & Emotional Well Being ~ you have sense of ease and comfort being with others that are close to you and being yourself.

Education ~ at school or at work you are confident in your level of understanding and knowledge and "fit" within your team or class.

Finances ~ you have obtained a sense of comfort with the amount of money you earn and not a "preoccupation" of "keeping up with others."

Faith / Religion ~ you have reached of level of comfort in practicing your faith and are comfortable with the people that surround you in your faith.

STEP 4: Esteem and Mutual Respect

At this level of development and evolution there is less agitation and "dis -ease" with others and yourself. I refer to it as "being comfortable in your own skin." While Maslow focused on the need for "esteem" and "esteem from others," I would like to refer to this as "mutual respect."

At this level of esteem you begin to feel comfortable with yourself, which allows you to be more comfortable with others.

There is a great lesson at this level of development that I think is the transition toward a more evolved life. Rather than being narcissistic and self-absorbed there is the realization that what you give is what you receive. "Treating others as they would treat you."

Relationships ~ you are "comfortable in your own skin" and comfortable with others and the various levels of friendships you establish without feeling threatened or judgmental?

Physical Being ~ You understand the level of work and effort needed in order to take care of the physical gifts you have been given and are consciously aware of how to maintain it. You and others admire your sense of fitness, but not egotistically.

Sexuality ~ intimacy is a gift that you value and understand the essence of mutual satisfaction as a friend and lover. You do not feel the need to force intimacy in order to get what you want or desire or use sex for manipulation.

Mental & Emotional Well Being ~ you have an ease of handling stress, anxiety and pressure. You have found stability and homeostasis when interacting with others.

Education/Work ~ you are satisfied with your level of accomplishment and understanding of what you know and what others know. You are not "threatened" by those that potentially know "more than you," but rather respect those that are knowledgeable.

Finances ~ money represents a "means to an end" and not a constant preoccupation with accumulation at any cost. You are comfortable with what others around you earn and what you earn as a living.

Faith / Religion ~ you have a comfortable knowledge and respect for your faith and are an active member of your "religious" community and have the mutual respect of those in your faith.

As I stated earlier in this book, I do not disagree with Dr. Maslow's ""Hierarchy of Needs" and this is why I have not renamed or relabeled, but rather enhanced or added to his hierarchy.

Dr. Maslow was the creator of the concept of being "self-actualized." Living a fulfilled life or as I have referred to it, "becoming the very best U that U can be." There are many variations of this same thought throughout history and certainly in the modern day "motivational movement."

In Dr. Maslow's book, *"**Toward A Psychology of Being**"* published in 1968, he wrote this about "self-actualized" people;

> *"Self-actualizing people, those who have come to a high level of maturation, health and self-fulfillment, have so much to teach us that sometimes they seem almost like a different breed of human beings."*

Dr. Maslow conducted a great deal of study and reviewed what he called, "Peak-Experiences," by "self-actualized" people. I would compare this to the experience athletes and performers now call "being in the zone."

In, "the zone" maximum performance is almost effortless. Right, almost impossible to imagine, but if you ask people that have had "peak performances" or state they have been "in the zone," they will explain to you that their maximum effort almost seems effortless. Their performance was extraordinary, whether it be in a sport or theatrical production or musical performance. They enter this space where there is such intense focus that the ordinarily challenging act or performance seems almost effortless and yet from a fan's perspective it looks as though there is extra effort or intensity, resulting in a perfect or peak performance.

This leads us to "Step 5" and the achievement of "self-actualization" or "fulfillment." I stated earlier in this book that I am not a psychologist, psychiatrist nor do I have a doctorate in psychology. Nor am I the perfect man. Nor have I lead an exemplary life and have myself reached fulfillment or "self-actualization." In fact, in writing this book and conducting all of my research and reading, I have found myself lacking in many areas and have a long way to go toward "self-actualization" and "Becoming the very best that I can be." So, it would seem that these steps are for all of us to follow, including me. And I hope that as you take these steps toward your own fulfillment you will help others understand the journey toward enlightenment and fulfillment, because I cannot imagine a greater calling than to help others embrace their own beauty and potential and help them to live a life of fulfillment and "self-actualization."

STEP 5: Self Actualization ~ Fulfillment of One's Potential:

If there were an easy way to live a "fulfilled life" then a majority of people would probably be doing it.

When you close your eyes and envision being "self-actualized," fulfilled or "becoming the very best U that U can be"... what do you see? What do you feel?

How do you think it will feel when you can look at yourself and where you are, at whatever stage in life that it occurs to you, that you have truly reached a sense of "fulfillment?" "Self-Actualization." Not just in one aspect of your life, but in many if not all aspects of your life.

Relationships ~ you are not only "comfortable in your own skin," but you have drawn people into your life, that contribute to your health and well-being and you contribute to theirs. There is no sense of intimidation nor threat of insecurity or betrayal.

Physical Being ~ Regardless of your age, you have developed your body into peak condition and physique. You respect and enjoy your body for the magnificent machine that it is and you take care of it as need be through proper exercise and nutrition.

Sexuality ~ regardless of your sexual preference, you have no need or concern of what others think or judge based on your personal sexuality and how you express it in a loving way with a mate or partner in the privacy of your own relationship.

You understand and appreciate the patience and blessings of desire, passion and satisfaction with the one you love.

Mental & Emotional Well Being ~ stability. You have perfected the balance of your emotions and the impact that they have on your mental state. You have found balance and acceptance in how you process information and conduct yourself in a mature and respectful manner.

Education/Work ~ you are satisfied with your level of achievement. You do not need to "prove" anything to anyone professionally or academically. You have maximized your ability to process information that contributes to your knowledge of life and your role in it and how to share that knowledge to help others, but are not threatened by people that potentially know "more" or "different" things and feel unthreatened by the knowledge of others.

Finances ~ you have earned a significant income that satisfies the needs of your life and has provided you with a lifestyle that fulfills your wants and needs and supports your family.

Faith / Religion ~ you have reached a level of seniority or knowledge of your faith and are seen as an "elder" or respected for your position within your "religious" community.

FROM THE AUTHOR ~ IN THE END

In the end, we are all one species and one gene pool.

We have been given the gift of life with all of its beauty and all of its challenges.

We, as a species have created terrible atrocities against each other and we as a species are not evolving at the level we are capable.

Dr. Abraham Maslow's *"Hierarchy of Needs"* is a profound introduction into the development and evolution of a human being and we have not used it properly. Businesses have used it more effectively to sell us things and take our money than education has used it to help our children evolve at a faster pace and have a better understanding of self.

I have developed the *21st Century Multidimensional Hierarchy of Needs* to provide a more complete view of Maslow's original hierarchy and breakdown in its easiest form directions on how to acknowledge where you are currently and how to take steps to change it.

It is time to *"TAKE ACTION TO MAKE THINGS HAPPEN!"*

If you are living a life of "quiet desperation" or with the mentality of "same shit different day." It's your time to read this book and every other book that tells you how to change your life and live up to the amazing potential that you have been given.

I was once told, "it's the lovers that lose." I didn't understand. It's not the physical "lovers," but rather the "lovers of things." People that love with passion can create great highs, but get hurt so deeply with terrible lows.

You cannot live this life in fear. Give everything you can to be the very best that you can be, every day and hopefully you will reach the day of fulfillment and "self-actualization" and know it was all worthwhile.

About the Author

Kevin L. McCrudden is the son of Irish immigrants and the youngest boy in a family of eight. He is a twin to Karen, number eight. He is husband to Alicia and father to Kevin Thomas, Harrison and MaryKathryn.

He is President of Motivate America, Inc.; Founder of National Motivation & Inspiration Day; Creator of the American Motivation Awards and Publisher of Soccer Long island Magazine.

His passion and love for America comes from his immigrant parents instilling the belief of the "American Dream" and that America is the greatest country in the world and that anything is possible here.

On December 18, 2001, after the tragic events of September 11, 2001, Kevin became the *only* motivational and leadership speaker in America to have a day of recognition passed by The United States Congress acknowledging the importance of "motivation and inspiration" in our daily lives. H. Res 308 were sponsored by United States Congressman Felix Grucci and several other members of Congress.

This resolution gave birth to National Motivation & Inspiration Day, which is January 2nd of every year and the beginning of Kevin's journey to help Americans and young adults to "become the very best U that U can be !"

Kevin has experience as a stand out High School and College athlete, professional athlete, certified mediator, candidate for public office, management and sales trainer, motivator, national speaker, husband, brother, son, parent, lover, friend and now, author.

He is an ordinary American man with an extraordinary American dream.

AudioInk Publishing

AudioInk Publishing, a division of Made For Success, Inc., is dedicated providing authors and speakers the opportunity to make their books, eBooks, audiobooks, speeches and mobile apps available to leading retailers worldwide.

Visit our Website: www.AudioInk.com

Get Quantity Discounts

AudioInk products are available at quantity discounts for orders of 10 copies or more. Please call us toll free at

(888)-884-8365 x 5 or email us at service@madeforsuccess.net.

CPSIA information can be obtained at www.ICGtesting.com
Printed in the USA
BVOW070224170912

300504BV00001B/7/P